Pathways
to Teacher
Leadership

Pathways to Teacher Leadership

Emerging Models, Changing Roles

MARYA R. LEVENSON

Harvard Education Press

Cambridge, Massachusetts

Second printing, 2018

Library of Congress Control Number 2013951064

Paperback ISBN 978-1-61250-654-8
Library Edition ISBN 978-1-61250-655-5

Published by Harvard Education Press,
an imprint of the Harvard Education Publishing Group

Harvard Education Press
8 Story Street
Cambridge, MA 02138

Cover Design: Deborah Hodgdon
Cover Photo: Jorg Greuel/Digital Vision/Getty Images

The typefaces used in this book are Adobe Jensen Pro and ITC Newtext.

This book is dedicated to my mentors—
my mother, Ann Randall,
and Patricia Albjerg Graham
and Tom Sobol—

and to my grandchildren—
Callie, Eve, Eliza, Abe, and Emmett.

CONTENTS

viii CONTENTS

FOREWORD

IN *PATHWAYS TO TEACHER LEADERSHIP*, Marya Levenson expands our understanding of teacher leadership. She shows how teachers learn to take leadership roles, not only *instructionally*, but also *institutionally* and in *education policy*. She engages us in a deeper look at each of these areas of leadership by helping us understand the various contexts in which teachers emerge as leaders—including charter schools and traditional public schools, teacher-led schools, and turnaround schools—and by examining the complexities that each of these leadership roles creates.

Levenson deftly guides us through a thicket of social, political, and educational issues with her own critical eye—never romanticizing teacher leadership, but rather offering an important alternative to the current "shame and blame" game in which teachers are held responsible for all the problems in education. She explains why teacher leadership is important and what it looks like in these various contexts. In a variety of authentic settings, we hear the teachers themselves tell us not only *how* they learn and lead, but how their world changes as they take on new responsibilities.

For example, the book follows two teachers as they become instructional leaders—one by introducing *action research*, the other by creating interdisciplinary *critical friends groups*. In each example, the teachers learn how to engage large numbers of their high school faculty members in their respective activities. Levenson reminds us, however, that both teachers have difficulty labeling "poor" teachers because of the power of the egalitarian ethic that pervades teaching that assumes that all teachers are alike—and that all teaching is the same.

What about teacher leadership in charter schools? Levenson explores this as well. Many teachers in these small urban schools are young, yet they are quickly involved in the challenging task of helping to create schools, regardless of their teaching experience. They are still learning to teach even as many of them are thrust into leadership roles. Levenson explains why learning to teach and learning to lead often come too fast for people to handle both at once.

Most educators know about teachers who lead instructionally, but few recognize the intentional and influential role teachers can play in changing the culture of the adults in their schools. Levenson introduces us to teachers who take on institutional leadership roles in their schools. Some do it by their involvement in union activity, and some are able to cross administrative boundaries yet stay involved with their peers even as they take on administrative responsibilities. Some teachers lead informally, while others have formal leadership positions. Levenson also explores teachers' roles as mentors, department chairs, and others who assume leadership with a direct focus on affecting the culture of the school when it is in need of change. And she looks beyond the classroom and school settings to the emerging influence of teacher leaders on education policy.

Pathways to Teacher Leadership asks the key questions about teacher leadership—not only how it works and what the examples teach us, but the fundamentals of recognizing teachers as leaders in a variety of contexts. Can these various roles be sustained? Will teachers accept other teachers in leadership positions? What do principals need to do to support teacher leadership? How can they build the kind of trust needed for teachers to accept teacher leadership? And how can aspiring teacher leaders learn to navigate the political waters of their schools' cultures?

This book is full of jewels—examples, questions, reflections, advice, and the insights of thoughtful teachers who are willing to examine their leadership practices. It is a piece of scholarship, even as it often reads like a novel. In short, *Pathways to Teacher Leadership* is a fine addition to the field. It offers a critical understanding of teacher leadership that can help us move toward authentic school reform.

—Ann Lieberman
*Senior Scholar, Stanford Center for
Opportunity Policy in Education*

ACKNOWLEDGMENTS

THIS BOOK was written with the help of teacher leaders, principals, researchers, and leaders of nonprofit organizations. (Wherever possible, I have used pseudonyms to obscure the identities of the teachers, principals, and the schools in which they worked.) I want to thank the following educators for their dedication and leadership: Jill Harrison Berg, Berta Berriz, Komal Bhasin, Annie Blais, Kelley R. Brown, Lizzy Carroll, Beth Cullinan, Betsy Drinan, Sarah M. Fine, Kim Frederick, Brian Goeselt, Jonathan Greiner, Deborah Holman, Liana M. Kish, Dennis Klem, Jenna Laib, Rebecca Lewis, Ambrizeth Lima, Pei Pei Liu, Karman Mak, Paul Martenis, Kaitlin Moran, Vito J. Perrone, Jennifer Price, Paul Roman, Larissa Showalter, Gillian Smith, Francesca Stark, Josh Wiczer, and Lonnie Yanesurak.

The Ford Foundation generously provided funds to support the work that Professors Chris Bjork, Sam M. Intrator, Cheryl Jones-Walker, Lisa Smulyan, and I have been doing to develop urban teacher leaders. Seventeen urban teacher leaders (mostly graduates of Consortium for Excellence in Teacher Education [CETE] colleges and universities) came together for several days during two consecutive summers to learn about the challenges and opportunities of urban teacher leadership. They also received individual support and some mentoring in regional meetings during the year. Thanks to Darline Berrios, Daniel Braunfeld, Stacy Carlough, Tom Chen, Beth Gourlis, Liza Hansel, Joy Kogut, Sarah Langer, Steve Lazar, Jennifer Lunstead, Sarah Marchesi, John McCrann, Kathleen Melville, Caitlin Moore, Becki Norris, Scott Storm, and Rachael Thomson, dedicated and reflective urban educators who shared their thinking and experiences. I am also grateful to Sarah Birkeland, Katherine Boles, Celine Coggins, Ann Cook, Helen Featherstone, Sharon

Feiman-Nemser, Susan Moore Johnson, Larry Myatt, Meghan O'Keefe, Nili Pearlmutter, Heather Peske, Phyllis Tashlik, Vivian Troen, and Judy Ullman, who have shared their thoughts about their work with teachers.

I have learned so much from the scholars whose work helps me to understand the history and issues surrounding teacher leadership. A sampling of their excellent work can be found in the Additional Reading section at the back of this book. I am indebted to Professors Tara M. Brown, Kristen Lucken, Joseph Reimer, and Mitra Shavarini, members of my writing group, and Caroline Chauncey, editor par excellence, who helped me clarify my thinking and prose. Finally, I would especially like to thank Andy Hawley, my husband, editor, and partner.

Teacher leadership is based on the premise that teachers have [an] integral stake in and responsibility to participate in the direction of the school, that teachers are involved in the school just as they are involved in their own classrooms.

—MICHAEL, a teacher leader in a New York City school

INTRODUCTION

THIS BOOK IS WRITTEN about and for teachers who are taking leadership in public schools. It is also written for the administrators who support teacher leaders, whether formally or informally. It is based on the recognition that teachers and principals are the central actors in school and classroom improvement, and that the school reform enterprise has much to learn from them. By capturing the stories of actual teacher leaders and their principals, this book shows how we can empower teacher leaders within and beyond schools and enable their voices to be heard.

Teachers enter the profession with the desire to inspire their students to become engaged learners. In my experience, they are usually the first to welcome knowledgeable supervision and support that would help them improve their practice. Today, however, many have become cynical and wary about the consuming accountability requirements implemented each year by states or central offices, and the "shame and blame" tone that permeates discussions of school reform. As Dennis, a high school teacher, noted recently, "It's so hard to have to spend my time proving I'm a good teacher, instead of becoming a better one."

It might surprise those who think of teachers as defenders of the status quo to see how eager many teachers are to take on leadership

responsibility and explore new roles. Indeed, a growing number of teachers refuse to make the choice between working with students and working with peers. In part this reflects a generational shift among the teachers
in our schools. The so-called next generation of teachers does not neces-
sarily plan to make a career in the classroom. Many envision teaching
for six to eight years and then moving on to some other role—whether
in schools, in other areas of education, or in a different field altogether.
Historically, schools have offered few opportunities for career growth for
ambitious educators. The emergence of teacher leadership is both a prod-
uct of and a response to this new trend.

A second trend that has contributed to the growth of teacher leadership is the increasing number of teachers working in mission-driven
small urban schools, many of them charter schools. Typically these
schools recruit novice teachers who may have little formal preparation,
and assign them unprecedented levels of responsibility given their limited experience. The long hours and intense demands typical of these
kinds of schools require a level of dedication that many teachers find hard
to sustain over time. Teachers in these schools grapple with the demands
of leadership. While many of them leave after several years of teaching,
others seek ways to better balance their work in the classroom with their
roles as leaders.

Most books about teacher leadership focus exclusively on instructional leadership. I prefer to use a broader definition: teachers are leaders when they act to improve instruction, strengthen the culture and
organization of schools, or speak out on policies and practices that
affect schools.

As figure I.1 illustrates, most teacher leaders are focused on improving instruction. A somewhat smaller group focuses on institutional
leadership within the school. A third, fledgling group of teacher leaders
is beginning to raise its voice about education policy. The overlapping
circles reflect that educators who want to be institutional leaders must
first have credibility as effective teachers in the classroom, and those
venturing into the policy realm must understand how the instructional and institutional aspects of the school function separately
and together.

FIGURE I.1
Teacher leadership

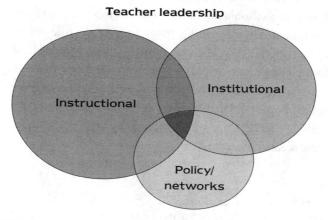

Teacher leadership

Instructional

Institutional

Policy/
networks

INSTRUCTIONAL LEADERS

Instructional leadership is most often the primary focus in discussions about teacher leadership. The first and second chapters of this book describe educators working in this arena who are exploring questions about student learning so that they and their colleagues can become more effective teachers. Instructional leaders might conduct classroom research, make their instructional practice public through rounds or team participation, and/or mentor beginning teachers and coach other colleagues. As Joan, a high school administrator, noted about instructional leaders at her school: "What they value is their classroom work, their curriculum work, and the kind of dissatisfaction with the status quo in their classroom. They're very hungry for change, and they keep revising and changing things and sharing with colleagues."

While the first chapter examines instructional leaders who are second-stage teachers with four to ten years of experience in larger, more traditional schools, the second chapter focuses on instructional leadership asked of beginning teachers in small urban schools.

INSTITUTIONAL LEADERS

Secondary teacher leaders, in middle or high schools, may find themselves drawn into schoolwide issues to better meet the needs of students and/or adults in their learning communities. While some are self-appointed, others are part of an appointed "distributed leadership" team that is formed when a principal delegates or distributes some of the tasks that administrators might otherwise perform. Teachers in these roles are described in chapter 3. Chapter 4 takes up the role of principals in supporting teacher leadership, and chapter 5 looks at emerging models for formalizing teacher leadership.

LEADERS ADDRESSING DISTRICT, STATE, OR NATIONAL EDUCATION POLICY

This emerging arena of teacher leadership is the least frequently discussed. Although traditional views of teacher professionalism find it difficult to reconcile the politics of the policy arena with the educator's role, some entrepreneurial reformers have demonstrated no such hesitation, encouraging teachers to be critical about the status quo. Technology has also enabled teachers to communicate across districts and states. As policies become increasingly intrusive in the classroom and school, more teachers are turning to networks to speak out about instructional issues and to raise policy questions. These efforts are described in chapter 6.

This book grows out of my work as a teacher and school leader, and as a teacher educator mentoring emerging teacher leaders. It draws on conversations and interviews with teacher leaders at various stages of their careers. Since the dynamics and expectations around school leadership vary with school context, the teachers interviewed include those in larger, more traditional schools as well as those in smaller urban charters or mission-driven public schools.

Because there has been much less written about teacher leadership in middle and high schools, the focus of this book is also on secondary schools, which are seen as the most challenging level to reform in K–12 schools.

I will consider the following questions as I examine teacher leadership in the three arenas:

- What encourages teachers to take initiative to provide leadership? (Some of the teachers in this book have consciously appointed themselves as leaders; others were surprised to be identified as teacher leaders.)
- What challenges and opportunities do teacher leaders face in different school contexts?
- How can principals support teacher leaders, and what are some of the dilemmas and tensions involved?
- What are some emerging models for teacher leadership, and how are they being implemented?
- What avenues are teachers developing for speaking out about education policy?

MY OWN JOURNEY AS A TEACHER AND LEADER

I first became interested in teachers and leadership in the late in 1960s while I was studying to become a teacher. I had the opportunity to study with Professor Paul Nash, who wrote *Authority and Freedom in Education*. I also worked with others to create the Boston Teachers Center, a place where teachers could learn from each other, raise questions, and express their concerns during a time of political activity when questions were being raised about the role of schools in our society.

In 1971, I became a ninth-grade history and civics teacher at the William Barton Rogers Junior High School in the Boston Public Schools and taught there for three years. With the beginning of desegregation, I transferred and became part of a dedicated group of teachers and administrators who created first Brighton High Annex and then Madison Park High School, a Boston magnet school. After participating in an anti-war caucus in the Boston Teachers Union (BTU), I was elected to the union's executive committee. When I later served as an assistant to Dr. Robert Wood, the superintendent of the Boston Public Schools, I was able to organize one of the first initiatives that brought together teams of teachers and their principals from the Boston middle schools. After my doctoral program at the Harvard Graduate School of Education, I became an administrator—first as a high school principal in Newton,

Massachusetts, and then as the superintendent of the North Colonie (New York) School District. Each year as superintendent in this district educating more than 5,000 students, I would interview every teacher that committees recommended that we hire, because I felt that selecting teachers and orienting them to the culture of our district was one of the most crucial components of my work.

Since my appointment as Professor of the Practice in Education at Brandeis University in 2001, not only have I had an opportunity to teach undergraduate and graduate students interested in education, I have also had the opportunity to work again with Boston-area teachers. With support from the Arthur Vining Davis Foundation, the Brandeis Education Program began to offer induction assistance to any teacher in the Boston area who had graduated from one of the undergraduate teacher education programs in Consortium for Excellence in Teacher Education (CETE) schools. We gathered teachers each month for dinner, and the A. V. Davis funds enabled us to provide mentoring for teachers in their classrooms for several years. (CETE colleges and universities include Barnard, Bates, Bowdoin, Brandeis, Brown, Bryn Mawr–Haverford, Connecticut College, Dartmouth, Harvard, Middlebury, Mount Holyoke, University of Pennsylvania, Princeton, Smith, Swarthmore, Vassar, Wellesley, and Wheaton colleges and universities.) The eighteen CETE undergraduate teacher education programs affirm the importance of the liberal arts as a framework for preparing reflective teachers dedicated to inquiry and social justice.

Even after the funding and classroom mentoring ended, the Brandeis/CETE monthly dinner meetings have continued, and they enable graduates from CETE colleges who are teaching in the Boston area to meet. Teachers who attend the voluntary monthly dinner meetings are self-selected educators who come to reflect with colleagues about challenges in their teaching and schools. They work in urban (charter and traditional) and suburban schools. Casey and Kalinda, two of the teachers in this book, chose to participate in this induction program for several years. As novice teachers, they found the network a safe place to vent about their schools. Having a confidential setting where it was safe to speak honestly about interactions at school was so important to some participants that they refused to bring colleagues from their schools to the meetings!

The Brandeis/CETE network began by offering only monthly dinner meetings where beginning teachers could reflect on their experiences in a safe and supportive setting, but after a couple of years, we found that we needed to differentiate the support we were offering. Therefore, I started an urban teachers' meeting that convenes five times per year. And as many of the CETE teachers wanted to continue to participate even beyond their first years, my colleagues Ned Rossiter and Sandra Resnick and I had the pleasure of mentoring young people as they developed into teacher leaders.

As my Brandeis colleagues and I observed and supported these young educators becoming teacher leaders, I noticed different patterns of teacher-principal interactions and teacher leader development in various school contexts. Members of both the more inclusive and the smaller urban groups expressed much frustration about school administrators and culture, which interested me as a former administrator. Wanting to understand these interactions better, I realized that I would have to learn the perspectives of both teacher leaders and their principals in order to work more effectively with teachers facing many challenges in their schools. I therefore developed a research project about teacher leaders that I was able to pursue during a sabbatical.

I began my research with a focus on CETE alumni, but soon included other teacher leaders and principals in my research. I conducted semistructured interviews with three different groups of educators. The primary group included teachers and principals in four charter or alternative small urban schools (two in Massachusetts, one in New York City, and one in California), a large suburban school in eastern Massachusetts and a smaller working-class suburban school in western Massachusetts, a Boston pilot school founded and co-led by two teachers active in the Boston Teachers Union, and a middle school in Ohio led by two teacher leaders. (Approximately half of these teachers were graduates of CETE education programs.) The second group of educators involved seventeen teachers who participated in a CETE Teacher Leadership for Urban Schools institute during the summers of 2011 and 2012. (These participants were interviewed before and after their participation in the institute.) The third group interviewed was comprised of colleagues who have been supporting and/or researching teacher leaders.

Ten of the twenty-nine interviews I conducted were with graduates from CETE colleges and universities. Because I was interested in the impact of school culture and context, whenever possible I interviewed teacher/principal pairs in the schools in order to understand how and why teacher leadership might differ across these contexts. The interviews, which lasted approximately an hour, were taped, transcribed, and coded. Coding was based on teacher leadership research as well as on themes that emerged from the interviews, and I used cross-case analysis to identify major themes. In my interviews with teachers, I examined their preparation as teachers, their definition of teacher leadership, their reasons for taking initiatives inside and outside their classrooms, their accomplishments, and the kind of support that they wanted and/or received from their principals. Interviews with principals focused on their career paths, their definition of teacher leadership, and their perceptions of the challenges and positive outcomes in developing and working with teacher leaders. I asked both groups about incentives needed to support teacher leadership. In follow-up interviews with both teachers and principals, I explored their understandings of power and influence in schools.

The teacher leaders and their principals whose thoughts and actions are reported throughout this book affirm that one size of reform does not fit all. Varying school contexts create challenges to the notion of establishing common expectations for teacher leaders across urban, suburban, and rural schools. Teachers and principals who have worked in a school for a while understand its specific history and culture—the context in which new initiatives are introduced. Each principal also plays a major role in supporting or discouraging dedicated and reflective teachers who want to assume leadership roles. School leadership, culture, and context matter.

I discovered that these educators are not inspired to take on the additional responsibilities of leadership because of a financial incentive (although they wouldn't turn down a higher salary). Nor are they responding to an external mandate or a desire to earn a higher numerical score based on a "value added" designation about their students' progress. Rather, these teachers are driven by internal motivation and their beliefs about working with others in a learning community to improve teaching and learning for all students. Moreover, although this book examines teacher leaders through the three lenses of instructional, institutional, and policy frameworks, many teacher leaders do not describe the tasks and functions they perform as discrete and separate. As Francesca, an experienced teacher leader in Brookline, Massachusetts, notes, "Teacher leadership is about moving teaching forward: doing your job to expand and deepen the profession."

I am indebted to these teacher leaders with their passion, dedication, and wisdom as they work together to improve schools, especially those that serve our most needy students. We have much to learn from their stories. It is my hope that this book, with its stories about teachers leading inside and outside schools, will add to the conversation they have begun, and to the growing knowledge about teacher leaders' roles in a learning community.

The teacher leader demonstrates a deep understanding of the teaching and learning processes and uses this knowledge to advance the professional skills of colleagues by being a continuous learner and modeling reflective practice based on student results. The teacher leader works collaboratively with colleagues to ensure instructional practices are aligned to a shared vision, mission, and goals.

—Domain IV, Teacher Leader Model Standards[1]

1 INSTRUCTIONAL LEADERSHIP

Learning to Reach Beyond the Classroom

INSTRUCTIONAL TEACHER LEADERSHIP is an essential part of improving student learning, recruiting and retaining strong teachers in struggling *and* affluent school districts, and creating a more inclusive vision of the profession for the twenty-first century. Thus we begin this book by exploring the different ways that secondary school teachers develop as instructional leaders in various school settings. Chapter 1 focuses on instructional leadership in traditional secondary schools; chapter 2 examines such leadership in charter and other small urban schools. We will discover how instructional leaders not only support the learning of students and fellow teachers, but also challenge some of the traditional assumptions about teachers and the teaching career.

Until recently, teaching professionalism was understood as the autonomy that a teacher possessed to decide curriculum and instruction after she closed the classroom door in order to educate her children. Aside from some educative mentoring for beginning teachers and rare classroom observations, most secondary school teachers did not receive much instructional feedback from colleagues or even from supervisors. (Unlike secondary school teachers, elementary school teachers sometimes received support from literary and mathematics coaches, who worked with their colleagues to introduce new curricula and resolve instructional challenges. Many of these coaches, however, have disappeared in large cities as a result of budget constraints.)

The advent of the standards movement has affected not only students' learning, but also teachers' work and evaluation. Reformers have worked to shift the K–12 paradigm about professionalism from that of an autonomous educator who decides about curriculum and instruction in her classroom to a teacher working with colleagues to focus on what Richard Elmore calls the instructional core.[2] Moreover, because of recent state policy changes flowing from the Race to the Top initiative, principals and/or department heads are being required to observe every teacher for at least ten to fifteen minutes several times a year. Teachers are being held accountable for the progress or value-added scores that their students attain on standardized tests during the academic year. Yet even in this vision, there is recognition that it is the individual teacher who will make and implement instructional decisions, especially those that relate to the students in his or her classroom.

There has not been much change, however, in the paradigm of the secondary school teacher's role. Typically the secondary school teacher works in a classroom by herself and is rarely supported to discuss either instructional challenges or accomplishments with peers. Most high schools do not offer opportunities for reflective teachers to share with colleagues what they have learned about teaching and learning, or to contribute to a more nuanced understanding of how to implement education reform. This isolation undoubtedly contributes to the fact that almost one third of beginning teachers leave the profession during their first five years. As Susan Moore Johnson and Morgaen L. Donaldson have noted, the predominant culture of a flat teaching profession, where first-year teachers have the same teaching responsibilities as those who have been teaching for twenty-five years, still discourages teachers from standing out.[3] Nonetheless, some second-stage teachers, who have taught for four to ten years and are respected as strong teachers, may be eager to assume instructional leadership roles.

This chapter tells the stories of several exemplary teacher leaders who have demonstrated informal or semiformal instructional leadership in traditional secondary schools. In the absence of formal, negotiated roles with clear expectations, these teachers have carved out roles and evolved different ways of relating to colleagues. The first story focuses on a teacher who chose to do action research in her classroom, and how her initiative spread throughout the school. The second story examines how a large suburban high school supports instructional leaders to reflect together on teaching and learning.

Almost all instructional leaders at one time or another have mentored beginning teachers. Sharon Feiman-Nemser has written about the steep learning curves beginning teachers face in their first year or two of teaching; they need educative mentoring from teacher leaders and opportunities to participate in induction programs where they can get help with pedagogical challenges they are facing in this vulnerable early career stage.[4] New educators should not have to discover by themselves how to teach during the first couple of years in the profession. After all, we want beginning teachers to do more than survive; we want them to be able to become respected professionals who choose to remain in schools. Teachers should be able to thrive in their chosen profession by deepening their knowledge and skills as passionate, inquiring, and effective educators who:

+ Are knowledgeable about the subject/s and the larger context in which they're teaching;
+ Care about, motivate, and challenge the individual children in their classrooms;
+ Are reflective about what works and what doesn't in the varying classes where they make hundreds of decisions each day.

This chapter examines how teacher leaders can go beyond mentoring beginners to begin raising questions about how experienced teachers can learn from each other. Teacher leaders can provide wisdom, perspective, and even a sense of humor about effective ways to implement new reforms. Many principals, acknowledging that they cannot bring about instructional reforms by themselves, increasingly are asking teachers to assume more instructional leadership. They are turning to teachers with more instructional expertise as the faculty develops and implements new curricular standards and assessments. Richard Elmore notes that "there is no other way to improve instructional practice in schools than to organize groups of adult learners to work on problems of instructional practice and to weave those groups into an organization-wide strategy of improvement. The evidence is clear on this point."[5]

As teacher leaders move to demonstrate leadership, they face questions about their relationships with colleagues and supervisors. In some ways, this is uncharted territory. Anthony Bryk and Barbara Schneider have written about the importance of recognizing power differentials and developing relational trust among teachers, principals, students, and parents in order to improve education offered to struggling urban and rural children.[6] Such skills in managing human relationships and politics are not, however, automatically taught as part of teacher preparation; each of the teacher leaders in this chapter has had to learn how to maneuver successfully through her or his school culture. Their stories show that not only do teachers receive different messages about when or how they should explore leadership roles, they also need to learn whether the schools in which they are working are more or less welcoming to significant instructional changes. Thus, we will read that varying school cultures call forth different kinds of instructional leadership.

» MADDY

Action Research in a Rural/Suburban School

Meet Maddy, who is working in a high school with approximately 500 students in western Massachusetts. This high school is in an older, working-class community where generations of families have attended the school, while recently more professionals have been moving in. Maddy says that the school culture is rooted in the community:

Our students show a level of respect and politeness that connects back to the [working-class] culture of the town. There is limited risk taking academically ... students are not trained to self-advocate in the same way that they are in some of the more affluent communities in the area. There's a sense of community here. The teachers really look out for students. Our survey results, as well as my own experience, show that the vast majority of our students feel like they have adults who care about them and who look out for them. In that way, there's also a certain level of pride in the school community.

Maddy has been teaching here for ten years and is very much a part of this school community, where she has made strong connections with the high school students, her peers, and the neighborhood the school serves. A well-respected second-stage teacher who has survived the challenges of learning her craft as a beginning teacher, she heads the social studies department and serves as coordinator of professional development at the school. Maddy has not only established her credibility as a very fine teacher, but she has also consciously developed a nonthreatening, diplomatic way of sharing her expertise in curriculum and instruction with her colleagues, who do not always welcome new initiatives or what they perceive as educational fads.

While Maddy is firmly rooted in this school, she also chooses to be an active participant in teacher networks outside her school, which puts her "more in touch with reflective practice and the bigger educational picture." Her ability to be both an insider and an outsider, her combination of closeness and perspective, has helped her to be effective at knowing how and when to introduce some curricular initiatives. As you read her story, you will notice that it took a while for Maddy to model for and then encourage her colleagues to try action research, which has enabled many of her colleagues to be more reflective about teaching and learning in this small high school.

Maddy grew up in what she describes as a "working-class culture." Her mother was a kindergarten teacher, and her father was an English teacher before he joined the National Guard during the Vietnam War. Maddy did well in school and ended up in a small liberal arts college in western Massachusetts where she did not feel she fit in, because many of the other students had attended private high schools or secondary schools in affluent communities. As an undergraduate, she got involved in a youth program—working on youth empowerment with young people in a neighboring urban community. She said: "Finding that niche for myself was really important, because I felt like a fish, sort of lost in the sea when I first started there. So, this was a way for me to find a place within that school." She eventually became a trainer of other college students who wanted to do tutoring in a Latino community that was not their own. One day, the director of the program asked her: "Why wouldn't you become a teacher? You have the ability to do that, you have the power to do it. You can go to school to get your certification. You can access so many more kids than you would ever be able to access through this work."

Maddy followed this advice and entered a teacher preparation graduate program, where she once again became involved in a community service learning education program. Those who know her now may think that Maddy is a natural leader who easily became a tutoring site coordinator, organized a conference, and developed training for the student tutors so that they could learn about cultural competence. She feels, however, that she was continually juggling being an insider and an outsider in a culture and institution where she did not feel she belonged.

Maddy has mixed feelings about her two years in the University of Massachusetts Amherst teacher education program, but she did learn that "unless you decide to educate yourself by trying and practicing in the classroom, you're not going to learn to be a good teacher." After substituting for a year, Maddy entered the high school where she now teaches. She soon realized that this was a culture that was familiar, but that she still needed to adapt.

> When I first came here, probably for the first five years, teachers had to be able to fit into that working-class culture, even though some of our teachers did come from professional families. Teachers need to be able to engage and converse within the community and be accepted by the students . . . People who couldn't interact with the staff and the students in a comfortable and respectful way left.

She was able to fit into the school's culture, partly because her "theory about learning is that the people who've been teaching for a very long time have a great deal of knowledge to teach us. I wanted to learn from them. For me, it was never about how I was going to come in and show how I knew everything." Maddy also brought a reflective approach to her own teaching. She thought, "Okay, if that didn't work, how am I going to fix it, and how am I going to make it better?" She decided that her first task was to learn her craft and establish herself as a strong and caring teacher.

The veteran teachers grew to know and like Maddy during her first years of teaching. They were willing to support her desire to create a new course after her first year of teaching. The new course, entitled "Power Play: An Introduction to World Politics," became quite successful and popular. After three years of teaching, Maddy began to look beyond her classroom and to think about how she could contribute to the larger school community. She became part of the Five College School Community Partnership program in western Massachusetts. She also participated in professional development through the Boston Center for Collaborative Education. When she won a teaching award in 2006, a new district curriculum director asked her what she thought they should do for curriculum development.

Maddy believed that if it was a top-down initiative, it was not likely to succeed in this school. Instead, in 2008–2009 she began to explore action research, which enables teachers to identify a problem of teaching or learning in their own classrooms, to collect data, and then to try different pedagogical strategies to address the problem. Proponents of action research work to merge theory and practice through their classroom research. Lieberman and Miller describe teacher action research as a form of reflective practice.[7] As Maddy was "trying to figure it out," colleagues in her department gradually became interested in what she was doing. She told the new curriculum director:

> I think that we need to create some kind of model where teachers get to initiate their own ideas, they get to do some research on their own, and they get to test out the stuff that they are looking at . . . We started trying to figure out action research by doing it.

Interest in this inquiry-based approach gradually spread from the history department to colleagues in other departments, and was eventually adopted as a schoolwide professional development program.

> We asked teachers to volunteer possible topics for the year. Teachers then self-selected into groups, and we required everyone to choose an implementation strategy. My group took Doug Lemov's *Teach Like a Champion* book, and chose one strategy out of that. We were looking at the concept of positive framing. We were surveying kids on their impression of some of the aspects of positive framing in the classroom . . . Each of the teacher research topics had to have a new [instructional] strategy that they would measure in the classroom. The strategy needed to be research based. They had to, at some point along the way, look at student work collaboratively within their group. At the end of the year, all groups did a presentation of their research findings.

After three years, what started as one teacher examining her practice about teaching and learning has spread across various departments in the entire school; the teachers in this school have become much more reflective about their practice and how to improve student learning. The instructional culture of this school has become more collaborative as teachers engage in monthly discussions of teaching and learning dilemmas with their colleagues. The very fact that they are willing to discuss their own instructional practice with colleagues has also changed how these teachers think about their teaching; reflection with others has become part of the school's professional expectations. All of the teachers chose to participate in one of the following groups in 2010–2011: Techno Tsunami: Technology in the Classroom; Teach Like a Champion: Positive Framing; MCAS Target Vocabulary; Guidance: It All Adds Up; Six Thinking Hats; Understanding by Design; and Teacher Toolkit for Inquiry-Based Research.

Maddy continues to cultivate her skills as a teacher leader. Her participation in the Five Colleges School Community Partnership network, a regional teacher network, gives her opportunities to share in "interesting conversations" and to get support and perspective outside her school. She does her best to keep up with current research and to share it in a nonjudgmental way. She says to her colleagues: "This is really cool. It's worked for me, and I'd be glad to share it." She has seen that this kind of embedded professional development has been effective in ending some of teacher isolation as well as in changing the school culture. Teachers feel greater ownership of what they are doing:

> Teachers are no longer sitting in a room full of people, correcting papers while someone speaks to them for two hours, and then not doing any-thing with that information . . . They like the fact that they're testing stuff, that they're actually getting a chance to talk to each other. We're getting a chance to hear what each other is doing instructionally, which is some-thing you just don't have the opportunity to do, because people are always too busy telling you stuff.

Students are also being challenged to take more academic risks. Aca-demic requirements and rigor have increased over the past fifteen years. Maddy notes: "I really push my students hard a lot because I push myself hard. I think that they need to be taking risks and trying new things. I'm always willing to try new things. So, I expect them to try new things."

Why does Maddy take on this teacher leadership in addition to her teaching load? She says:

> All of the work that I do significantly improves my teaching. It feeds me as a teacher and keeps me thinking. It pushes me to try new things. The daily grind had moved me away from the philosophical aspect of teaching, and I now feel integrated again.

Although there is much stability among this school's teachers, there have been three principals at the school in the last decade. The newest principal is supportive of the action research initiative, but it is clear who is the leader coordinating the initiative. The principal, who described himself as "being callow in this role," said that it was "huge that I saw [teacher] leaders in the building and could strike up col-laboration with them." He recognizes that Maddy is a leader who has earned the respect of veteran colleagues and provided some instruc-tional continuity throughout the changes in school administration.

What skills and dispositions does Maddy think enable her to be an instructional teacher leader?

> I am more than willing to speak up at any moment when I believe that the young people in my school are not getting the support that they need. I think that's an attribute, just being willing to take the risk and put yourself out there to advocate for students. I work really hard all the time, and I do my best to keep up on current research and thinking about teaching, pedagogy, and what works in the classroom. I try to help other teachers as much as possible by sharing new resources and new opportunities, but in a way that doesn't suggest, "Hey, I know what the best thing is for everybody. So, you should probably listen to me." That is not how I feel, and it's not helpful to think that way. We're responsible for the students in our school as a team.

Despite the leadership experience she had before she began as a teacher, it is very unlikely that Maddy could have initiated significant changes outside of her classroom in her first or second year of teaching. She had to earn personal and professional credibility (and learn how to teach) before she could lead the action research initiative; she also had to learn about and be respectful of her school's culture. Although she is now a department head and the professional development coordinator for the school, she continues to be respectful of her colleagues; she does not think or act as though she is the fount of all knowledge.

Maddy herself needs instructional nourishment inside and outside of her school so that she can continue to grow as a reflective educator. Her participation in the Five Colleges School Community Partnership network sustains her and enables her to be in touch with new developments in the profession so that she can be a trusted liaison among the classrooms, the school, and the larger educational community.

» NORTHERN HIGH SCHOOL CRITICAL FRIENDS GROUP
Collaboration (and Its Limits) in a Suburban School

The second example of teacher leadership describes a kind of instructional collaboration that is possible in Northern High School, a large, affluent Boston-area suburban high school where the administrators and teachers are committed to teacher leadership. Samantha ("Sam"), the principal, envisions her role as providing vision and direction for the school, and resources such as time for teachers to meet to discuss teaching and learning. Joan, the vice principal, is a former teacher in the school whose main duties center on instructional leadership. She introduced interdisciplinary Critical Friends Groups into the school as part of a small learning community initiative. Critical Friends Groups (CFGs) meet each month and use protocols to discuss the work of either a teacher or a student. Although the group's name seems to describe an activity where teachers are critical of each other, CFG protocols are actually designed to help educators consider essential or "critical" challenges of teaching and learning in a safe, structured democratic group. According to the National School Reform Faculty website, the purposes of the Critical Friends Group are to:[8]

- Create a professional learning community
- Make teaching practice explicit and public by "talking about teaching"
- Help people involved in schools to work collaboratively in democratic, reflective communities (Bambino)
- Establish a foundation for sustained professional development based on a spirit of inquiry (Silva)
- Provide a context to understand our work with students, our relationships with peers, and our thoughts, assumptions, and beliefs about teaching and learning
- Help educators help each other turn theories into practice and standards into actual student learning
- Improve teaching and learning

At Northern High School, teacher leaders acknowledge and model the importance of their work. As Charley, a history teacher leader said, "We're doing something very, very important here. And if we don't do it right, it has profound consequences for our country."

Since most previous research on teacher leadership has focused on elementary schools, researchers have not written much about the impact secondary school size can have on teacher leadership. In a large suburban high school, the faculty members cannot all sit around one table, or even three or four tables; as a result, they usually find themselves relating primarily to colleagues within their department or organizational units, such as houses or schools within a school. A school's size thus has a significant impact on structural and human relationships among teachers and leaders.

Large secondary schools have developed different ways of encouraging communication among teachers. In a middle school, teams or clusters of teachers hold weekly discussions about the students they have in common; teams and clusters also make it easier to plan and implement interdisciplinary units. In a large high school, departmental units play a similar role; they encourage teachers to collaborate around content and instructional questions with their colleagues. It is rarer for high school teachers to work with colleagues in other departments. Because course schedules are not usually built with an eye to interdisciplinary work, it takes a special effort to cross departmental lines for joint teaching (unless the school is structured around interdisciplinary humanities and mathematics/science blocks of time, as some schools are).

In this suburban high school with approximately 150 teachers for 1,800 students, teachers usually relate more to their department chairs than to the school principal. In some ways, Northern is an unusual school, because Joan is a vice principal who explicitly requested that her responsibilities include finding ways to carve out space for teachers to examine together issues of pedagogy that engage and challenge them. Joan, who is slight in stature, is very warm and welcoming; she is also very clear about her beliefs and determination to achieve goals that she and others have selected. She began by initiating voluntary interdisciplinary CFGs for teachers who wanted to work with colleagues as part of an initiative to create small learning communities.

As these CFGs gradually evolved into departmental groupings, Joan and Sam, the principal, decided to devote resources to support and institutionalize the groups. Sam and Joan struck an interesting balance while trying to change the culture in this suburban school. Rather than simply allowing various departments to establish (or not) collaborative teams, the two school leaders made it quite clear that such teams *would* be established according to a model for collaborative learning in which teacher leaders who continued to have full-time teaching responsibilities would be appointed as teacher leaders to convene teacher teams.

Sam, Joan, and the department heads were able to provide some resources for the instructional teams. Joan "strongly believed at the time (and still does) that a team needs a facilitator to prepare the agenda, to keep the group on track, to learn some skills in facilitation, to learn some methods of discussion which might include how you look at student work and get data from it." They carved out time in the schedule for teachers to meet each week in groups. They were able to relieve teacher leaders of a weekly administrative duty as a signal of the importance of teacher teams. Joan also wanted to protect CFG or team meetings so that they did not become consumed by administrative tasks. She provided a sympathetic ear and suggestions for the instructional team leaders when they found themselves confused about how to handle resistance or personal conflicts among members of their teams.

A teacher is appointed to lead weekly conversations with colleagues according to content areas. There are teacher leaders for biology, chemistry, physics, English, and history, and other departmental teams whose responsibilities are to support discussion about curriculum, instruction, and assessment, as well as some mundane logistical and organizational tasks. These educators, who are respected colleagues trained as facilitators, lead these instructional groups. The teachers meet at a regular time each week. Establishing these groups within departments has made it easier to institutionalize them because they parallel an existing structure in the high school.

The two principals pursued a delicate balance that combined a schoolwide expectation that instructional teams would meet each week to focus on student learning with the recognition that, given this school culture, teams needed to have flexibility about how to develop and achieve specific instructional and learning goals. Confidentiality was encouraged within team discussions so that teachers could open up about their questions and vulnerabilities without fearing how such sharing would affect their evaluations. Meanwhile, team leaders were expected to share the topics discussed and the general tenor of discussions with their department chairs, who did not attend the team meetings.

It was the department chairs (rather than the teacher leaders or colleagues) who continued to have sole responsibility for assessing the quality and effectiveness of teachers. Although the state's high-stakes student assessments caused teachers to articulate and coordinate their curricula within their departments, the instructional teams' sharing of some instructional approaches did not challenge the cherished autonomy of the teacher in his or her classroom. Most of these teacher-led discussions were framed around sharing best practices or ways to resolve instructional dilemmas so that the participants could decide whether they wanted to adopt such an instructional approach. One exception to this voluntary approach occurred when the science groups decided to develop a common midyear assessment so that they would be able to diagnose and support students who were struggling with the content.

The departments and instructional teams vary in how they have established a culture of reflection. As David, a mathematics teacher leader, notes: "This department is known to be pretty collegial ... It doesn't mean that everybody is going to take and use everything that everybody shares, but nobody is tightfisted with their own creation." Other departments are not perceived as this open. Regardless of the departmental character, educators are pleased to be teaching in this suburban school, with its collaborative culture that also encourages individual initiative and creativity.

In this school, second-stage teachers are tapped to fill instructional leadership roles. The team leaders, who are selected by their department chairs in coordination with the vice principal, have what we might call semiformal roles. They are released from one administrative duty (such as supervising a study hall), but they do not receive additional pay. Nor are they seen as part of the administrative team. The process of agenda setting seems to vary somewhat by department, with some teacher leaders consulting closely with their department head (who does not attend these weekly meetings), and others creating the agenda from topics suggested by colleagues. Charley described this as a "top-down collaborative mandate." At a time when curriculum often seems dictated by the need to prepare students for assessments created by those outside the school, having the authority to decide what will be the focus of their team's reflective deliberations is important to these teachers. Charley noted, "It's really fun as a teacher to sit down and begin a discussion about what were our teaching goals for the unit, take a look at the content we brought in, and then how successful we were in achieving those goals and measure that by looking at examples of student work."

Why do the informal instructional leaders do this extra work in addition to the many demands facing a teacher each day in the classroom? Teacher leadership roles enable these educators to have a voice about instruction; they want to create and participate in a learning community where teachers reflect on their practice. These semiformal leadership positions also provide recognition for teachers' accomplishments in a flat career path. One teacher noted modestly that there is not a big divide between his own teaching effectiveness and that of his peers, but several acknowledged that their sense of competence is affirmed when their department head or principal asks them to do leadership work. Thus, Paul, who is a science teacher, also serves as a mentor for beginning and experienced colleagues. "People come up to me and ask, 'How does this particular concept go?' I guess I'm seen as an authority contentwise. I have the teaching experience. I really am also interested in education research. I read a bunch."

Although standards-based learning and state assessments have pushed these suburban educators to be less autonomous, they appreciate opportunities to articulate their own learning goals and develop shared departmental assessments. For example, one of the science teams has lively discussions about the pros and cons of assigning more challenging or easier science assignments to classes where students apparently have different abilities. These teachers have developed some common student assessments that are modified each year so that the students do not hand down the questions (and answers) to the incoming classes. The group spends much time discussing which test questions to develop and use. Not only do they work hard to find out if the exam questions are actually assessing the skills and knowledge they have taught, they also have a close working relationship with a teacher of English language learners who helps them "diminish the window dressing" that might confuse students struggling with the English language. In addition, they analyze the student data from state tests and department assessments each year to see whether they should be teaching some concepts better.

In this suburban school, educators must teach for six or seven years before they are recognized as instructional leaders. Because it is the norm for teachers in suburban and rural schools to wait until they become more experienced, second-stage teachers before they speak up, challenging this norm may bring some criticism and pushback. In fact, David recounted how a more veteran teacher reacted when he spoke up in a departmental meeting during his third year of teaching: "I don't know what I said, but one of my coworkers made a comment. She said, 'You know, when a weed gets a little too long, the rains have to kind of settle it down.'"

All of the teacher leaders interviewed in this school expressed interest in what they were doing and pleasure in working with colleagues to consider instructional issues. Despite the CFG training and support, however, these experienced teacher leaders were not sure whether or how they should challenge weaker colleagues or those who did not want to collaborate. It is true that this school's hiring committees tend to recruit and select teachers who welcome such a collaborative culture. There are still unchallenged boundaries, however, based on longstanding concepts of teacher autonomy, that remain very strong in this and most school contexts. For example, Paul, one of the science teacher leaders, has been unable to get peers to observe and give feedback to their colleagues about their instruction. When he suggested that they observe each other, "all of a sudden, people just couldn't find the time to do that." Even though most of his science colleagues share classrooms and are in and out each day to get equipment, "somehow, suddenly having somebody just sit there and actually watch was something people didn't want to do." He did note that "it's hard to sit there and watch another class when you know that you've got piles of papers and things to do."

Paul acknowledged that even in a department with a culture of sharing instructional strategies, as well as of developing and implementing a common midyear and final assessment, "there's so much counterpressure from doing [such observations]" because of a longstanding culture of professional autonomy, which Dan Lortie has described so well.[9] Susan Moore Johnson and Morgaen L. Donaldson describe the impact of this longstanding culture:

> Teacher leaders' efforts to share their expertise can also be undermined by the culture of teaching. In fact, the professional norms of teaching present a daunting challenge to teacher leaders who are asked to improve their colleagues' instruction. Our interviews suggested that colleagues often resist these teacher leaders' work because they see it as an inappropriate intrusion into their instructional space, an unwarranted claim that the teacher leader is more expert than they, and an unjustified promotion of a relative novice to a leadership role. Thus, the norms of autonomy, egalitarianism, and deference to seniority that have long characterized the work of teaching remain alive and well in schools.[10]

These suburban second-stage teachers believe that it is not their responsibility to confront peers who are not teaching well. Although some of them might discuss their concerns with their department chair, others feel that they should not breach the confidentiality of the weekly discussions or their peers would never feel comfortable opening up about their vulnerabilities. David, one of the teacher leaders, was clearly bothered by this, as he recounted:

> It's getting to the point where this [really weak] teacher will be tenured, and then she'll be there forever. And I don't think anybody knows . . . So, I don't know how much of it is my job to take that on, except to push the fact with the person that this is a common curriculum that we teach, and the expectation is that we've gotten through it.

Whether educators can support and assist teachers while also assessing them has been an ongoing debate in education. As we will read in the next chapter, charter and some alternative schools now expect teacher leaders to be able to do both. (Peer Assistance and Review programs also are built on the expectation that both functions can and should be combined.)

When we compare the culture of this affluent suburban school with the previous smaller school serving a more working-class clientele, it appears that teacher leadership has been built more into the culture and organization of this larger school, although with limits on the teacher leaders' authority. The principals have incorporated teacher leadership by making yearly appointments of very qualified educators within departments who are responsible for leading small group discussions about teaching, learning, and assessment while focusing on how to engage all students. These regular conversations offer important opportunities to ask questions, share successful strategies, and reduce some of the professional isolation found in traditional schools. Joan is also aware from her own experience that some of these talented and experienced teachers need new challenges if they are going to stay in the field. She remembers what she and some other strong teachers were feeling in their sixth to tenth years of teaching:

> There was a collective plateauing. We were really good, but we looked at each other and said, "Okay. Now who's pushing us?" Where's the mechanism or the structure to work with like-minded peers, younger or older, experienced or less experienced, to really push your practice and your work?

Because she was wary about going into a traditional administrative role, Joan welcomed the opportunity to be part of a planning group when the school administration decided to develop teacher leaders. She soon realized that, just as beginning teachers need to have mentoring and induction as they learn to teach in their first year, many of these experienced teachers also need to learn new skills in order to become educative mentors and leaders in instructional areas. In addition to offering training to Critical Friends Group leaders, the vice principal and/or department head is available to consult with teacher leaders as challenges arise. There is thus internal institutional capacity to help develop and support these teacher leaders in their new roles.

What these instructional leaders are not willing to do, however, is challenge the traditional boundaries about teaching autonomy in the classroom. Teachers remain reluctant to observe each other, and the teacher leaders in this large, successful suburban high school are uncertain about how or whether to proceed when they confront or hear about poor teaching. These unclear professional boundaries puzzle some teacher leaders as to what their role should be when they face colleagues who do not want to collaborate or are less successful in the classroom. We will see that there is no such uncertainty among the teachers in the small urban schools we will visit in the next chapter.

REFLECTIONS

Teachers, especially second-stage teachers who have mastered the beginning challenges of teaching, may choose to extend and broaden their focus beyond the children in their own classrooms by examining practice and research with colleagues. Some conduct classroom research or make their instructional practice public through "rounds" or team participation. In addition to mentoring beginning teachers, instructional teacher leaders often seek to open classroom doors and overcome some of the isolation in their own classrooms.

Opening the door to a classroom requires trusting relationships among the school's educators. Bryk and Schneider have written about the need for "relational trust," which must be developed before teachers are willing to share their vulnerabilities and questions with colleagues.[11] If teachers are worried that sharing concerns will later become part of a poor evaluation, they would be foolish to be honest about their problems. If, on the other hand, educators believe that their colleagues and school leaders have integrity, are ethical and competent, and are focused on how to improve student learning, they can create a school culture where teachers will take the risks involved in examining their practice with others. In such a culture, teachers are often willing to assume the additional responsibility of instructional leadership.

As we read the stories of instructional leaders, we may observe that there is an interaction between how the instructional leader defines herself or himself and the school culture, or "the way we do things around here." Lieberman and Miller describe the need for teachers to lead in communities of practice where individuals "go public with their work, have it scrutinized by their peers, improve it, justify its use in relation to a local or statewide set of standards, and present their teaching to an audience of peers."[12] The informality of secondary school teacher leadership requires that teacher leaders must develop the "consent of the governed," even in cases such as a Critical Friends Group where there is institutional support. Teachers interested in leadership need to be able to understand the often unstated norms of the schools in which they are working so that they can be effective working with others.

The instructional teacher leaders described in this chapter are reflective educators who have retained a spirit of inquiry about teaching and learning, and a passion for their profession. They are hungry to learn more effective ways to educate their students. They are willing to try new instructional strategies and learn from their mistakes. Even after they work long hours teaching and correcting lab reports or papers, they somehow find enough energy to take a graduate course, read some research, or go to workshops. They continue to ask questions about their students and about themselves as educators. It is helpful that the administrators in the two schools in this chapter provided some consistent time and training for second-stage teachers who wanted to explore teacher leadership. Teacher leaders repeatedly describe the need for teacher leadership time that does not come on top of a full load of teaching.

Second-stage teachers gain status and credibility among their peers through their willingness to reflect on their teaching practice. Teachers often resist or are cynical about implementing the instructional reform de jour. Instead, as this chapter indicates, instructional leaders have to have enough confidence to be honest and vulnerable about the results. They reflect on whether what they are doing works or does not work to improve teaching and learning. Such thoughtful reflection is usually welcomed by their peers.

Yet even in these two schools, which were selected because of their commitment to teacher leadership, colleagues' resistance can make it a risk to speak out. Learning how to work with peers often requires acquiring different skills than those needed to become an effective teacher of adolescents. Instructional leaders need to understand how to swim among the fish—and the occasional shark—in their own school culture and context. Thus Maddy slowly earned credibility by becoming a respected teacher who first tried out initiatives in her own classroom and then generously offered to share what she had learned with her colleagues. Paul and other second-stage instructional leaders in the large suburban school had to gain recognition as effective teachers. They went to workshops and were mentored by their department heads so that they could learn how to be good facilitators of instructional teams in their departments. Although they are sometimes concerned about the competence of a few of their colleagues, they have learned not to challenge colleagues' boundaries re professional autonomy.

The instructional leaders in the first two school settings developed knowledge about when to introduce research or a different perspective to their colleagues. They learned not to give the impression to their colleagues that they were the fount of knowledge. In some ways, this refusal to acknowledge that some teachers may be more knowledgeable than others is a major limitation that arises from a long-held conceit that all teachers are equal in the profession. This perception arises not only from the unions' assertion that all teachers are equal members of a bargaining group, but also from the traditional male administrator's perception and treatment of female teachers as a passive group awaiting direction from the leader. We will note in the next chapter that this perception of teaching as a flat profession is being challenged as younger members enter the profession and reformers differentiate teacher roles.

... the prospects for teacher leadership remain dim if no one can distinguish the gains made for students.

—Judith Warren Little[1]

2 INSTRUCTIONAL LEADERSHIP IN SMALL URBAN SCHOOLS

No Time to Lose

IN CONTRAST TO their suburban colleagues, teachers working in charter or small mission-driven urban schools are often young people who enter teaching directly after graduating from college, often through alternative-route teacher education preparation. The young people who make a commitment to teach in these schools bring much energy and a sense of urgency to their work. They face high expectations and demands while working to catch their students up to where they should be in skills, knowledge, and social capital. Teachers in small charter and alternative urban schools are expected to teach and advise students for up to fifty to sixty hours per week, longer work hours than colleagues in more traditional schools. Moreover, even while they are learning to teach, some of these young educators are asked to assume leadership positions during their first or second year of teaching. This is one of the biggest differences between teacher leadership in these schools and in the large traditional schools described in the previous chapter.

There is a second major factor that differentiates instructional teacher leadership in charter versus traditional schools. Charter school educators challenge long-held beliefs that educators' professionalism equals autonomy to teach in the ways they choose in their classrooms. Not only do many charter schools develop curricula and instructional strategies that their teachers are expected to implement, but teachers in these schools without union contracts must demonstrate their effectiveness quickly, or they will not be hired to teach for a second year. These expectations affect the organizational culture of both students and adults. For example, while there are clear expectations about what both students and teachers should do, the constant push for student success on measureable outcomes within a very tight time frame creates stress among adults as well as among the young people in these schools.

In contrast to the second-stage, experienced instructional leaders we met in chapter 1, the two teachers introduced in this chapter were asked to become instructional leaders very soon after they began to teach in their charter schools. These young women are smart, caring, passionate, and dedicated to teaching urban students as a way of addressing inequalities in our society. They were excited and challenged to assume extra responsibilities, even though they did not have much leadership preparation. As you will observe, their two stories have different endings because of the match or mismatch between the teachers and their schools' expectations and cultures.

» CASEY
Becoming a Department Head as a Third-Year Teacher

Casey was a history teacher in a Boston-area charter middle school with very different expectations around the issue of classroom autonomy than those found in suburban schools. Although she had liked to play "teacher" all the time when she was younger, she often had been frustrated in elementary school, where she had had trouble with reading and spelling. Having experienced both negative and positive learning situations, Casey started to realize in high school that she could have an impact on others' learning. Becoming a teacher seemed to her to be a natural way to serve others.

A graduate of a Consortium for Excellence in Teacher Education (CETE) undergraduate teacher education program in Maine, Casey had a very challenging first year of teaching social studies in a central Massachusetts charter school that was experiencing confusion and chaos while it went through several administrative changes. After this discouraging beginning, she applied to and was accepted as a teacher in a fairly new Boston-area charter middle school where the school head was very interested in teacher initiative and leadership. She conscientiously worked on improving her craft in this new setting.

A year after she had moved to the Boston charter middle school, Casey was appointed chair of the social studies department. She was only a third-year teacher, much younger than the second-stage teachers typically appointed to be team leaders in more established schools. Such an early promotion is quite common in charter schools, where there is high teacher turnover. Teachers who are young and inexperienced are often asked to assume administrative or organizational responsibilities in addition to their full-time, demanding teaching assignments.

Despite this early promotion to department chair, Casey felt that her credibility as an instructional leader arose from her demonstrated instructional expertise rather than from a title: "I don't think that the title brings respect from your peers, and I don't think that title means that you have more of a voice in the school." Casey felt instead that her ability to encourage faculty members to try some new curriculum or means of instruction arose from her credibility as an instructional leader: "[An instructional teacher leader is] sought out as someone you go to when you don't quite know what to do. So, there's an interesting relationship between the competence in the classroom and having a voice in what happens in the school."

Along with her colleagues, Casey was focused on preparing her students for the state student assessments. The entire school was organized

around using instructional time efficiently, because these educators concluded that their students (73 percent low income, 48 percent students
whose first language was not English) needed much additional work in
the areas of skills and content in order to catch up with their peers.
Casey's students did perform well on the Massachusetts state tests (and
the school is recognized statewide for its students' test results), but test
preparation has not been a sufficient learning goal for Casey since her
first couple of years of teaching. She wanted her students to be engaged
in their learning; she insisted that her students learn how to think critically. After taking a course on teaching Great Books, she implemented
Socratic circles and questioning so that her students would examine and
challenge each other on their assumptions and thinking.

Just like Paul at Northern High, Casey enjoys spending time exploring educational research:

> I really enjoy reading and research and finding more ideas. I also enjoy
> trying to articulate what I'm doing well or what others are doing well . . .
> I start reading and then have a list of ideas to draw from. So, when peo-
> ple get stuck, I have myself and my coworkers, but I also have that back-
> ground list of ideas for other people as well.

As she became a more effective teacher, Casey found that newer teachers were looking to her for advice and support. She discovered that she
had a role as an instructional leader who was willing to share her ideas and
instructional methods:

> I think that [teacher leadership] sort of organically spreads to other peo-
> ple by just having an open door; other people realize that your ideas are
> working. When asked, [teacher leaders] just share their materials, their
> experiences, and their advice . . . I think teachers get their legitimacy
> by being good inside their classroom and being recognized as such by
> other teachers.

Casey demonstrated instructional leadership in multiple ways in
her school, including by mentoring beginning teachers. And in addition to welcoming colleagues to observe her and to share her educational

materials, she published two articles about her instructional practice in professional journals for teachers.

Casey received mentoring and support herself through her participation, with other urban teachers from regular and charter schools, in the Brandeis urban teachers' group. She also was tapped to participate in the CETE summer institute for urban teacher leaders. Through these experiences, she learned some political and organizational skills—such as how to differentiate her objectives into those that could be achieved fairly quickly versus those to be achieved and sustained over the long term—that enabled her to relate better to her colleagues and principal. Casey says, "I really enjoy being part of the CETE group, talking to other teachers, and learning a lot just by listening. It means that when there's a situation going on, I'm not limited to my own experience." As she developed into more of an instructional leader, she also became very involved in helping to shape the school's norms and expectations for students. Casey notes, "Those teachers that are good inside their classroom tend to feel more confident in voicing their opinions to administration." Casey also had a principal who was dedicated to meeting with and listening to each teacher's reflections on what was happening in his or her classroom and in the school at large.

Unlike the instructional leaders in chapter 1, who were reluctant to comment on peers' practice, Casey expected to speak to her peers in or outside her department if she observed instruction or other activities that could be improved: "When I think of teacher leaders, I think of who is a teacher at school who won't watch something and just sort of feel uncomfortable about it, but will go up to that person directly and say something and coach them on how to do it better." In many small urban and charter schools, respected and credible teachers, regardless of whether they are in a formal position such as that of department chair, are expected and encouraged to give instructional feedback to their peers. Casey's willingness to talk with colleagues about their practice developed out of an urgent desire to make instructional suggestions if there was a good chance that intervening would make a positive difference for student learning. This is definitely a change from the much more private instructional practice found in traditional schools.

Nor is she the only small school instructional leader I found who has this perspective. Michael, who taught for five years in a small alternative high school in New York City, said:

> On the teams, we share the same group of kids. We're going to be together as a group of teachers and with these kids for four years. We need to help each other be as successful as we can be as teachers, and help the students be as successful as they can be as students. So, whatever we need to do to get ourselves to a place where we can be honest with each other, we need to do that.

Because they are so focused on helping their students succeed academically, teachers in schools like these feel that it is their responsibility to speak to colleagues in order to help them become more effective teachers. They refuse to accept long-cherished teacher norms of professional autonomy and are challenging the longstanding limitations about what a teacher can say to a colleague.

Mission-driven urban schools frequently extend the school day and week and push their teachers to give 150 percent to educate all children; many of these bright and energetic young teachers devote their hearts and souls to the mission. Those, like Casey and Michael, who appear to have leadership potential, are quickly tapped for extra responsibilities and visibility. These young educators are affirmed by the number of parents who want to enroll their children in charter and/or alternative urban schools. The teachers, who work to have their students master skills and do well on the state assessments, describe a kind of adrenaline high they feel as they work toward this shared mission. (There are also costs to this stressful pace, as we will note in the next chapter, on institutional leadership.)

» KALINDA
A Clash of Expectations and Styles

It is important to recognize that not all charter or small urban mission-driven schools are the same. For example, some charter schools are so focused on student outcomes as measured by standardized tests that they become rigid about how the school functions. These schools have clear expectations about how teachers should teach (and students respond), and often do not seem very open to teacher suggestions about possible changes. Their approach to teaching appears to work well for some students and for rookie teachers, but it is not suited to teachers who wish to question or suggest alternative ways of teaching and learning.

Kalinda is a serious, hard-working, and caring young Asian American woman with a great smile, who has high expectations of her students and even higher expectations of herself. She grew up in the Midwest in the 1990s and learned to teach in an undergraduate teacher education program at Swarthmore College, where she was inspired by stories of inner-city teachers equalizing education. After teaching seventh-grade history and geography in a suburban school for four years, she decided that she wanted to teach urban students. She was hired to teach social studies in a high-performing Boston charter middle school (very different from the one where Casey taught) that was also recognized for its students' performance on state standardized assessments. At first, Kalinda felt reassured by the school's uniform ways of teaching and learning. She worked hard to follow the school's prescriptions, which included very structured ways of paying attention to a speaker and answering questions, silent passing in the hallways, and a curriculum focused on developing skills so that the students could catch up and do well on the state assessments. Kalinda was successful, as measured by her students' performance on standardized tests, and at the end of her first year, she was asked to become a department chair.

However, because she had been prepared in the Swarthmore teacher education program with its emphasis on inquiry, Kalinda began to be frustrated by the school's relentless focus on mastering basic skills without much emphasis on critical thinking. She knew that the students she had taught in the suburbs were being encouraged to use creativity and critical thinking in their social studies classes. Therefore, she decided, as a teacher and department chair, to introduce critical thinking to her students while also covering the prescribed curriculum.

This was not a successful experience. By the end of her second year in the charter school, she discovered that her students were so used to direct instruction, "that any type of freedom that was allowed was taken to extremes" by these middle schoolers. Kalinda also felt increasingly exhausted and isolated in the school as she raised questions about curriculum and instruction.

Kalinda decided to leave the school; she felt burned out because of her attempts to conform to the rigidity and high demands of the charter school while also remaining true to her own values. Although she considered leaving teaching, after a year of reflection and rest, she eventually found her way to a network of California charter schools where she discovered a philosophy and culture that matched her own. In this network she attended workshops about how to be an instructional leader, which helped her learn skills about working with colleagues. She also studied the research about how to make effective change in school organization.

Equally important, when she was hired to be an assistant principal for curriculum and instruction at one of the charter schools in this California network, she had the opportunity to work with Steve, a principal dedicated to developing social capital among the students and adults. This principal, eager to acknowledge Kalinda's real strengths, recognized that she also needed mentoring as a supervisor. Steve helped her understand that she needed to moderate her impatience and become more affirming when giving feedback to teachers. She eventually became so successful as a leader that, at the end of her second year, she was selected to become the principal of this charter school when Steve moved on.

Why was Kalinda so much more successful in this second charter school than in the first? Part of the answer may be developmental. Through her experience and reflections on what had occurred in both the suburban school where she began teaching and the first charter school in which she worked, she had matured. Reflecting on her experience at the first charter school, she realized that she had not wanted to be treated "as a child who has stepped out of line." Because of Steve's mentoring and the leadership skills she had learned, she also was able to have a better perspective and a sense of humor about the bumps in the road as she worked in the second school's affirming culture. Kalinda also acknowledged that "sometimes you have to leave in order to find a good fit and the right culture."

Beyond these personal development issues, however, the second charter school was a better match because its organizational vision and culture affirmed her core values. In hindsight, Kalinda wondered how her previous school could be considered innovative when it continued to resist insights from the teachers, such as how to restructure the beginning of the school year:

> It doesn't make sense. On the one hand, the leaders told us that, as teachers, we were the ones that made the school run, and that we were the most important part of improving student achievement. On the other hand, when we shared ideas that they didn't like, they just ignored our suggestions, or worse yet, dismissed the ideas by saying the ideas didn't fulfill the mission of the school. The leaders are stifling creativity by saying this is the way it's always been done, and we're going to keep doing it because it has worked.

In contrast to her experience at the Boston-area charter school, Kalinda was given opportunities to gain leadership knowledge and skills through the California charter school network's professional development programs. She also had an opportunity to work with Steve, who was skilled in developing human resources. This principal conceived of his work with Kalinda as helping her to become a leader who was able to inspire and motivate others to work together with an inclusive, shared vision of how to educate children.

It is helpful to acknowledge that educators in various charter schools have different beliefs about teachers and their roles in a learning community. Many directors or principals of charter schools have not gone through teacher or administrator preparation programs. In fact, charter school leaders often disdain traditional education programs because they think that they are not sufficiently focused on the need for fast, major reforms built on an entrepreneurial vision of change. Charter school teachers who want to move into school leadership may be advised to go to a business school rather than attend education administration programs for principals. Thus, some of these leaders give short shrift to organizational or teacher-raised issues, which they perceive as slowing down change. They are so focused on raising *student* achievement as measured by state standardized tests that they do not spend much energy thinking about what kind of institutional changes need to take place to develop and sustain *teachers* as adult members of a hard-working and demanding learning community

« « » »

Most charter schools are expecting all teachers to become leaders by assuming professional responsibility for having all of their students achieve. Katzenmeyer and Moller assert that:

> If teachers feel confident in their ability to be leaders, they will assume responsibility for the learning of all students. This single outcome from teacher leadership can affect teaching and learning throughout the school. Linking teacher leadership to efficacy in their classrooms can help teachers understand how they can touch the lives of more students.[2]

In agreement with this sentiment, Stephen Farr, chief knowledge officer of Teach for America, entitled his book *Teaching as Leadership: The Highly Effective Teacher's Guide to Closing the Achievement Gap.* Although every charter school teacher is expected to be successful with all of his or her students—a very ambitious goal—it is useful to acknowledge that some are expected to do even more. While the teachers themselves are learning how to be effective educators, they are also asked to be leaders of other teachers, including those who are struggling.

There are exciting opportunities available for young teachers who want to participate in a social justice and educational mission by working in a charter or small alternative urban secondary school. Unlike in traditional schools, where it is the experienced, second-stage teachers who are asked to become teacher leaders, in these schools relatively inexperienced teachers are encouraged and expected to lead. Young, talented graduates of elite liberal arts colleges become excited about the opportunities to contribute, but they soon find out that they face some daunting challenges.

The two graduates of liberal arts universities described in this chapter crafted their own ways to address the demands of their urban charter schools. In the first story, Casey learned how to meet the school's demands that students pass the state tests, but she refused to settle for narrow test preparation. While strengthening her own instructional repertoire, she found ways to insist that her students develop as critical thinkers. She was able to do this partly because of her participation in teacher groups outside the school, where she was affirmed in her goals and commitment to a broader vision of education for urban students. She also worked in a school where Asha, a principal whom we will meet in chapter 4, valued her teachers' perceptions and suggestions about how to improve instruction. Not all of the decisions and wisdom in this charter school were dictated from above.

Like other teachers in some charter and other small urban schools, Casey operated on a challenging and intense instructional timetable that did not permit her to ignore some colleagues' struggles. In this school culture, it was everyone's responsibility to become an effective teacher as quickly as possible. If this meant speaking critically to a colleague about his or her teaching, so be it. This challenge to teacher autonomy is a significantly different and positive change from the more traditional relationships described in chapter 1 that prohibit teachers from acting on recognition of their colleagues' ineffectiveness.

In the second story, Kalinda decided to leave her Boston-area charter school even though she was perceived as successful and had been promoted to chair of the social studies department. She became burned out and discouraged about trying to fit her educational vision into a much more restrictive, top-down culture and organization. She felt as though her knowledge and perceptions were not valued in that school community. While she was missed by the friends she had made, her leaving was not seen as a signal of a larger problem for the community; her school, like many charter schools, treated teacher turnover as "simply the price of doing business."

Kalinda was prepared to leave teaching until she found a charter organization that affirmed her educational philosophy and enabled her to develop leadership skills. The Partnerships to Uplift Communities (PUC), a nonprofit charter school management organization in southern California, offers teachers training in coaching techniques, workshops about organizational change, and the facilitation skills needed to be an effective coach. Working with approximately twelve charter schools, PUC has established fall and spring professional development days focused on "community practice," where teachers who are effective are invited to run workshops for other colleagues in the PUC school network. Recognizing teachers' leadership abilities and valuing their instructional expertise, the organization hopes to be able to build and retain strong instructional leadership in their schools.

Both Casey and Kalinda recognized that they needed to strengthen their facilitation and problem-solving skills. Although her principal tried to discourage her from doing so, Casey eventually decided to leave her charter school to earn a master's degree in instructional leadership at the Harvard Graduate School of Education. Kalinda, on the other hand, was able to learn supervisory skills before joining a new charter school in California, and then was mentored by her principal on-site.

REFLECTIONS

As we reflect on the first two chapters, we should first acknowledge that middle and high school teacher leaders are engaged in a wide variety of instructional leadership roles. Although they share a common focus on teaching and learning, there are several differences in these roles, including how wide a circle of influence the teacher leader desires or is willing to assume. At one end of the continuum shown in figure 2.1, an inspiring teacher may serve as a role model simply by welcoming peers into her high school classroom or sharing a particularly effective teaching strategy with a colleague. A teacher can also conduct research on his teaching and/or students' learning that does not appear to challenge the autonomy of the classroom. When that teacher shares or publishes the results of the research, he is inviting colleagues to examine and comment on his professional reflections: what works, what is less effective.

In the middle of the continuum, the teacher's expertise may be recognized more widely inside and/or outside the school as he mentors a beginning teacher, makes a presentation about action research, and/or leads a departmental team in examining an instructional dilemma. At the other end of the continuum, charter teachers such as Casey and Kalinda also

---

FIGURE 2.1

Continuum of instructional teacher leader roles found in secondary schools

Informal ➤ **Formal**

Respected classroom teacher	Teacher researcher	Literacy or math coach
Teacher who makes suggestions about professional development and/or school culture	Participant in Rounds or Critical Friends Group	Board-certified teacher
	Instructional team member	BTLRC collaborative course facilitator
Teacher willing to experiment with new instruction/technology	Mentor to beginning teacher	Member of T3 cohort
		Charter school teacher leader

---

expect to intervene if they think that their knowledge and perspective would be helpful to a teacher grappling with an instructional dilemma.

Second, there are significant differences related to when teachers assume instructional leadership. Maddy and the suburban Northern High instructional leaders were second-stage teachers who had earned credibility and respect as very strong educators. These experienced teachers were ready and eager to assume more responsibility and to step into leadership roles that would offer them new challenges. That was not the case with Casey and Kalinda, who were expected to assume leadership within their first or second years in charter schools.

In addition, the foci of the beginning and second-stage teachers are often quite different. It is hard to separate the teacher leaders' tasks from the schools in which they work. Thus, while teacher leaders in many charter schools have a laserlike focus on getting their students to catch up, gain skills, and pass state tests, many second-stage teachers in suburban schools have the luxury of being more reflective about deepening their own practice as they consider how to have all of their students engage in critical thinking and creative inquiries. (Whether this will change in the wake of value-added student results becoming part of all teacher evaluations remains to be seen.)

As we have seen, instructional leadership responsibilities are usually added on to what are already very demanding expectations in the classroom. Teachers in charter schools who have neither the experience nor the confidence of veterans may be asked to be effective teachers and role models for a diverse group of students who are struggling to catch up academically. (Although most charter schools educate fewer English language learners and children with disabilities than other public schools, there is still tremendous pressure for charter school teachers to ensure that all of their students learn and do well on state assessments.) At the same time, these young teachers often may not have the power or understanding necessary to change colleagues' instruction and/or to create a more affirming learning community in their schools. When they are continuously urged to lead and produce results in these schools, some become burned out and leave—stressed by demands to teach *and* lead without having sufficient training or a clear understanding of how to leverage change.

Charter schools, which continue to expect beginning teachers to assume such leadership roles, need to acknowledge the challenges created by these additional responsibilities and to offer increased support and resources to these young educators, as the PUC network does. The challenge for leaders in these schools is how to sustain and develop these passionate teachers so that they can eventually become knowledgeable second-stage instructional leaders available to mentor eager beginners. Kay Merseth notes that more than one charter school prizes youthful energy over longevity. For example, the administrators of MATCH, a Boston charter, acknowledge that the strain of balancing personal and professional demands can cause a teacher to leave:

> We lose teachers every year when teaching staff have children or they get married—especially when they have children. It seems to be really challenging trying to balance both here.[3]

Because teachers in small, mission-driven urban schools have raised questions about how to be able to have some work/life balance, some charter schools have created sustainability committees to try to address these problems. Leaders in those schools realize that charter school teachers should be supported so that they can run a marathon, not just a sprint.

Third, it is important for instructional leaders to be able to maintain their perspective and energy by participating in induction or professional affiliations inside and/or outside their schools. The instructional leaders in both the first and second chapters found that reading professional publications or websites and attending workshops helped them to be knowledgeable about current research, which they found various ways to introduce to colleagues. Maddy valued her participation in the Five Colleges School Community Partnership network, where she was able to join interesting conversations about teaching and learning. The teachers at Northern High School had Critical Friends Groups. Casey participated for more than five years in the CETE induction group sponsored by the Brandeis Education Program. Although Kalinda also participated for several years in the Boston-area CETE group, she found the PUC school network support more relevant and helpful for her work in the charter school. Thus, these teacher leaders were able to maintain the bifocal vision produced by being insiders who at times had the advantage of an outsider's perspective. This helped them to articulate goals for instructional change while understanding that such a process would require patience and persistence.

Both young women working in charter schools also found mentors who helped them learn how to manage within their schools' cultures and institutional demands: Casey from her principal, as well as from a CETE mentor outside her school; and Kalinda from the PUC network and the principal in her California charter school. Mentoring was critical to developing and retaining both of these instructional teacher leaders who were working so hard to master instructional and leadership tasks in schools that did not always match their own educational philosophies.

It is important to recognize that the issue of teachers having independent or countercultural perspectives can be even more of a dilemma in a charter or turnaround urban school, where the principal has complete power to select, retain, or transfer teachers. These schools have been structured so that the administrator has the flexibility and power to build a team with a shared vision about improving student academic performance. At the same time, having such power can tempt the principal to keep only those who agree with what he says and to dismiss those who don't. Those who wield such absolute power would be wise to encourage and to keep the voices of those who disagree with the leadership. Otherwise, there will be no opportunity to consider the concerns that teachers might raise before the implementation of an initiative.

Indeed, as instructional teacher leaders have discovered constraints or faced a lack of support for instructional initiatives, they have begun to think about how they can help shape school culture and institutional change, as we will read next in the stories about institutional teacher leaders.

I wasn't totally content being just on the ground in my classroom every day. It just felt like there were too many bigger things to tackle.

—MELISSA, teacher leader in a Washington, DC, charter school[1]

3 INSTITUTIONAL LEADERSHIP

Changing the Culture of the School

ALTHOUGH MOST TEACHERS remain focused on improving the instruction in their own classrooms, some educators become interested in addressing institutional constraints and obstacles to teacher leadership and/or student learning. Some of these educators raise questions about how teachers or students are being treated; others become concerned about how instructional and other goals are being implemented in their schools. As Casey, the charter school teacher introduced in chapter 2, noted:

> If you're going to work on changing the culture of the classroom, you have to work on changing the culture of the adults. I really do think that everyone I work with believes that what we want for our kids, we have to live first.

49

When educators become involved in institutional reform, however, they soon discover that working for such change is not a simple thing, and that they need new skills in order to be effective in this arena. In addition, these teacher leaders often find that principals and colleagues do not understand how this work may become so engaging and demanding that it can eventually affect how much time and energy the educators have to devote to their teaching. In this chapter, we will see that mentoring can help teacher leaders interested in institutional change to place appropriate limits on their involvement and also learn how to understand and survive political currents along the way.

Traditionally there has been a top-down hierarchy in most schools; policy has come from the administrators down to the teachers in a loosely linked system. Thus, there is a history of secondary school teachers who become interested in formal institutional leadership—as a way to improve the school's functioning and/or as an entry to becoming a principal or district superintendent. For instance, male educators were often encouraged to think about "moving up" into administrative positions with more status and better pay than teaching. In previous decades and to some extent in the present, teachers interested in institutional leadership have also become involved in teacher union activity in their schools or districts.

Many teachers, however, have typically had little voice or input in the direction or daily workings of the school. All too often, when teachers disagree with administrative decisions about scheduling or resource allocations, they report being ignored or painted as troublemakers. For example, Janet, an experienced teacher in a large urban school district, recounted that even though various principals appeared to consider her suggestions, they actually ignored what she suggested: "'Sure, Janet, another good idea. Thanks. Next.' That's how it felt to me a lot of times. You just weren't given the authority to move things forward."

Her colleague Maria noted that teachers who articulated strong opinions were threatening to a principal with a belief in the traditional top-down hierarchy:

> He never really liked me, because I was so threatening to him. This has been
> my experience with principals if you are an advocate for children . . . You're

supposed to go along with the plan, whatever the plan is, even if you're really good and smart and knowledgeable. You can help for a while, but if it ever comes up that your ideas are contrary to the plan, [you're ignored].

The way that some principals appear either to listen (but don't really) or to ignore suggestions can lead to much teacher frustration. As a result, innovative teachers have tended to retreat to their classrooms to work with their students, because they feel that they have autonomy and authority there. These primarily female teachers often shut their doors and work to create inclusive and welcoming settings in their own classrooms, where they have some control.

This chapter focuses on the informal and semiformal institutional teacher leadership that has developed in secondary schools. Some experienced teachers have ventured into this arena because they were motivated by a desire to give voice and support to underrepresented groups of students, parents, or teachers. Typically, these educators might become concerned about the lack of institutional support for inclusion of students with disabilities in their classrooms, or that a school's shift to double classes for English and mathematics in preparation for testing drives out experiential and arts classes that engage some students and keep them from dropping out of school. Others might become involved because they believe that students of color or gay and lesbian students don't feel safe in a school or feel that their perspective is not included in the curriculum. Also, beginning teachers in charter or small urban schools are encouraged to take on institutional leadership roles. When they do so, they can face different opportunities and challenges than second-stage teachers in suburban schools.

While institutional leadership may seem quite separate from instructional leadership, the two are closely related. Teachers' instructional competence gives them credibility when they raise institutional concerns. Many teachers who become involved in institutional issues do so because they are searching for ways to build a school community that encourages adults working in the school to thoughtfully examine teaching and learning, and to consider what's working and what's not working in their school.

As we read about teachers who have demonstrated institutional leadership, we will consider the following questions as to why some teachers pursue leadership options to improve a school's institutional culture and organization:

+ What characteristics or capabilities make teachers willing to speak up and take the initiative to create a collegial professional learning community?
+ Because informal teacher leadership opportunities seem to attract women educators, how do these temporary positions both provide opportunities for and impose limitations on those interested in leadership?
+ What kind of mentoring do teachers need to become effective leaders in the institutional arena?

The voices of the teachers heard in this chapter affirm that working with adult colleagues is not the same as teaching children. Although both situations require the ability to listen well, we will discover that educators who want to engage in making organizational change need to learn specific skills and knowledge.

» GRACE

Multicultural Advocacy at Northern High School

In the first decade of the twenty-first century, Northern High School was losing some of its teacher leaders; teachers who had begun their teaching in the 1960s or 1970s were retiring. Turnover created openings for new leaders within departments and the larger school, and younger teachers began to feel they needed to step up in order to maintain a school culture that they cherished.

A few found themselves being tapped for leadership within their departments. Grace, a tall, striking, and determined Irish mother of three whose multiracial family lives in Boston, began teaching English in a New York City charter school in 1991. After three years she left that school because it was "totally overwhelming," and moved to Northern High School, a Boston-area suburban school that had "kids from all walks of life." Grace's career continued to move between urban and suburban settings; she worked in a Washington, DC, charter school for two years before returning to Northern High.

Grace, who is now a very capable and respected teacher leader, remembers that when she began teaching in the suburban school, her department head would offer her opportunities to present at department meetings. Grace did present at the meetings, even though it felt a little tricky for a young teacher like herself to present to older colleagues. She continues to be grateful that her department chair and a couple of veteran teachers mentored her, encouraged her to take some risks, and allowed her to make mistakes.

In the mid-1990s, Grace was asked by one of her students of color to advise a Step Squad (a rhythmic dance and music drill team inspired by Step teams, which exhibit and compete at historically black fraternities and sororities).

> I had this kid in my homeroom who wanted to start a Step Squad. This was a student who hadn't made the cheerleading team and perceived it as a racial slight and was really put out . . . She was a smart person and was always going to do well no matter what. But I was concerned that she would disconnect from the school if someone didn't work with her and make her feel that the school did care for her. So, I did.

Grace's involvement with this one student expanded to caring about the entire squad. She stayed with the team every day after school for four or five years. Step teams from other schools were invited to perform at the school, and students of color began to feel that the school culture was visibly acknowledging them and becoming more welcoming. Although African American and Latino students together made up approximately 12 percent of the student population in this suburban school, there were significantly fewer teachers and administrators of color. Students were eager to find more adult mentors willing to listen and advocate for them.

In 1999, when a disciplinary event in the school became racial, the principal pulled Grace into his office, where there was a very upset young woman of color. The student eventually cooled down when Grace promised to organize a schoolwide forum where students of color would be able to communicate their concerns about how the school was treating them. During this crisis, Grace became a key player because she had credibility with both students and the administrators. She said: "Trust was placed in me. I didn't know I deserved it until trust was placed in me."

As a person of integrity who was a mentor and teacher to students of color, Grace could cross boundaries that the administrators, who were associated with discipline, could not. The students felt that they were able to speak honestly and critically with her because she was not a school administrator. At the same time, the administrators knew that Grace cared tremendously about the well-being of the school, which meant that they were more open to listen to her when she raised concerns. She provided a credible voice that could be heard by both the students and the administrators.

Throughout her career, Grace had been mentored by her department head, veteran teachers, and the principal. When she made mistakes at first, her department head enabled her to learn in a sheltered departmental environment. She gradually earned credibility by becoming a very fine teacher, supporting students of color with the Step Squad, and making presentations in her department. Her work enabled her to gain knowledge and a broader perspective. Perceiving that much of leadership is relationship based, she strove to find ways to work with people she didn't know.

It is important to recognize that Grace had access to formal power channels in the school only because the principal reached out to her and supported what she was proposing. The principal eventually encouraged her to move into a semiadministrative position as the assistant to the principal, although she continued to teach two classes. The principal was able to mentor her as a leader with a schoolwide perspective. She soon "found herself in charge of all sorts of things that no one wanted to deal with," such as scheduling the school calendar (including state testing), supervising campus aides, facilitating communications to the staff, assigning administrative duties, and addressing parking problems.

Even in this semiadministrative position, Grace felt that she "was only successful because people perceived me as a teacher. I was able to give voice to how we protect teachers and provide support." Although she had authority as the principal's representative, Grace believed that her credibility and usefulness continued to arise from being able to hear and articulate the concerns of students and teachers who felt that they were not being heard. She was effective because she could cross boundaries between adults and students, and between teachers and administrators. She reflects that, "I never knew I could do all these things. I was just glad that I had a job."

The size of this school (with almost 2,000 students) has an impact on the way relationships among the adults and students are structured. Most of the teacher leaders in the school report having very few direct professional interactions with the principal, unlike in smaller schools, where there is often regular communication and interaction between the principal and teachers. The department chairs act as intermediaries and funnels for the schoolwide deliberations led by the principal and vice principal. More teachers seem comfortable taking instructional leadership within a small group (such as a department), where they know the members of the group and understand the defined nature of the task. There is a gap, however, between the responsibilities a teacher has each day in the classroom and the kind of organizational challenges that the principal of a large school faces. Teachers may speculate or share rumors about some schoolwide issue, but few teachers are willing to risk acting as a go-between who tries to understand and work on those institutional challenges.

» LEE

Assuming the Role of Go-Between

Lee, who is also a teacher at Northern High, is the rare teacher leader who is unwilling to let rumors fester in this suburban school. After growing up bilingual and attending a large high school in Miami, she attended Wellesley, a woman's college, where she became certified to teach as an English teacher. When I approached her, she was reluctant to be interviewed, because she does not perceive herself as a teacher leader. On the other hand, she is one of the few teachers in this large school who is comfortable moving between her peers and the principal.

When [a prior leader] was principal, there were a lot of rumors always. It was terrible, and I hated it. People would talk about stuff, and I'd say, "Well, we don't know if it's true." And I would be at the lunch table and everyone's having a fit, and I would say, "I'll be right back." And I would just go in [to the main office] and get an answer, and come back and say, "It's not true."

Lee also assumed a leadership role by addressing a schoolwide problem concerning the low participation of Latino families in Back to School Night and teacher conferences. Remembering her own experience in an urban high school when she was not encouraged to apply to competitive colleges, she decided to take initiative when an administrator at Northern High complained that Latino parents would not come to the school.

So, I worked on reaching out to parents, got all their phone numbers, and actually reached them at home. We worked on invitations, created an evening that included dinner that all the kids helped cook. They helped make the invitations. We invited the principal and the department chairs. I was so pleased they all showed up. The parents came, and it was a really great night. I think we got to do it twice before I had kids, and then it passed on to someone else.

What gave Lee her sense of agency—that she felt she had the power to be a gadfly, to approach the principal, and to organize the Latino families? She is not sure herself, although she had worked previously as a teaching colleague of one of the administrators and felt comfortable approaching that person. While Lee had clearly demonstrated leadership, she was surprised when her department chair asked her to mentor a new teacher, because she was not sure what she would have to share. When asked whether her uncertainty might be gender related, Lee responded with laughter: "Yes, most of the men at our school have no problem with confidence!" Nonetheless, Lee continues to feel a responsibility to be a credible go-between by helping reduce rumors and strengthening the school culture.

Lee soon learned that assuming the role of the person in the middle could be quite demanding: "There's work that goes with it. To be seen as a teacher leader felt burdensome at times, because people would kind of look at me like, 'Are you going to take care of this?'" Periodically Lee would withdraw from playing this role because of challenges surrounding her teaching or the care of her young children.

When her children eventually became older, Lee decided to do a semester internship where she shadowed the principal, which "only helped me with my respect for my administrators and all the stuff that they are dealing with." This administrative experience also clarified for Lee that she is and wants to be a teacher. As she noted, "Honestly, I like to be liked, and you don't always get to be liked when you're the one in charge. It can be really lonely, and maybe that's what has always pushed me away from it." Lee is comfortable with having carved out a role as a communicator and mediator:

> I used to say to my department head, "I'm the wing man. I'm not the pilot, but I will be your wing man." I do think that's where my strengths are. People will talk to me, and then I can help the person in charge know, whereas they're not necessarily going to the person in charge.

Grace and Lee have been successful as two instructional and institutional teacher leaders in this large suburban school for several reasons. First, they are respected as very strong teachers who are working with students and families who need an advocate. And with the assistance of mentors and veteran educators who served as role models, Grace learned about how the school functioned and what she had to do to make institutional change. Lee has created her own informal role as communicator and mediator, appreciating the freedom to take on or step back from task-based initiatives, depending on varying demands in her teaching and personal life.

Although these experienced women educators were not always sure what they had to contribute, succeeding principals have encouraged their participation and contributions as talented and caring teacher leaders. The flexibility to assume teaching and leadership roles at various points in their careers has enabled Grace and Lee to move in and out of informal institutional leadership roles as they have strived to balance work and family responsibilities. Their experiences working to make institutional change have enabled them to learn about how the school functions and what challenges leaders face. In their various roles as teacher leaders, they have developed greater understanding and empathy for their administrators, even as they continue to voice the concerns of students and colleagues.

» KELSEY

Too Much Responsibility Too Soon

In contrast to the experienced second-stage teachers at Northern High, first- or second-year teachers in charter or small urban schools are often encouraged to take on institutional leadership. Many of them find it very difficult to say no. While it is flattering to beginning teachers to be asked to take on leadership roles, the combination of teaching and having responsibility for tasks outside the classroom can take over more and more of the teacher's waking hours, until it seems as though he or she has no private life at all.

Kelsey attended Boston University, where she was struck by the contrast between her own K–12 preparation and those of other students. Perhaps because she grew up in a rural school and felt much less prepared than her college classmates who had graduated from high-powered suburban or private schools, Kelsey approached the challenge of college as if she had something to prove. Despite what she perceived as insufficient preparation, Kelsey was able to graduate from college after three years. During a semester abroad in Ireland, she applied to and was accepted into the small and personalized Brown University Master of Arts in Teaching (MAT) Program. During her internship teaching history at a Providence, Rhode Island, charter school attended mostly by Columbian immigrant students, she became an advocate for a student who had a history of truancy. In addition to motivating this student to participate in her class, Kelsey accompanied him to court. She described this involvement with her student as a "life-altering experience" because she learned so much about the challenges one of her students was facing.

After completing her internship, Kelsey applied to a charter school that is part of a national network of schools for students who have failed in traditional high schools. When she was hired, she found a school going through many changes. The history department head left the school halfway through her first year, and the four beginning teachers found themselves without curriculum and supervision. Kelsey felt that she needed to speak up.

> We had a lot of ideas about how to fix the [classroom management] problems in our classrooms—both in the short and long term—but these ideas [wouldn't be] heard without someone speaking up. And . . . for whatever reason, [that] kind of fell to me.

One of the reasons she felt comfortable being a spokesperson is that Kelsey, unlike her colleagues from Teach for America (TFA) or other alternative teacher preparation programs, had had a year in a MAT program before coming to the school. She observed: "I felt that I had pretty intense training, and I wasn't just speaking to speak up. I was usually saying something that I thought had merit." Her principal affirmed her perceptions when she sought her out "on a couple of occasions to say this is the feeling I'm getting from the staff. Can you speak to this?" However, when Kelsey spoke up about the unrealistic expectations for beginning teachers—to be creating curriculum as well as making ten calls to students' parents per week and supervising students with demerits—the message was that the administrators should be the ones to raise such issues in a teacher meeting:

> [The administrator] felt that, having been at this school for three times as long as I had at that point, she knew what was up and what was right . . . The message was if you have something to say, you can say it to me privately instead of in the whole group.

Kelsey noted that her colleagues were "comfortable and happy being teachers and working on their craft," while she was "really interested in that [institutional] stuff . . . I put a lot of care into what I do, which helps make me really confident in what I do both in the classroom and when I'm speaking up." As a result, the colleagues in her department increasingly looked to her to raise issues about teacher expectations, especially when a new department head arrived.

Kelsey resisted when the new department head told her at midyear that she would be teaching literature of the French revolution during the fourth quarter. She told the department head that she had no background or preparation to teach it. When she was reprimanded about this response by the department head in a meeting in the principal's office, Kelsey "just let myself sit there and be reprimanded. I left, and I was like, 'I don't care.'" Although the principal eventually intervened and teachers were informed that they would be able to select the courses they were going to teach during the fourth quarter, this confrontation was a turning point for Kelsey, who felt that she had been reprimanded like a child for raising questions about her competency to teach a subject.

Kelsey felt much more successful about her initiative to create student activities that would improve the school culture for students. This charter school was serving students who had experienced failures and negative school interactions in previous schools. Because she observed that the aftermaths of disciplinary interactions in the school between young people and adults were seeping into the classroom and having a negative effect on learning, Kelsey decided to organize some extracurricular activities that would create more positive and trusting relationships within the school.

> The school was about academics all the time, and it was a very un-fun learning environment. [You] did not feel that coming to school was something you wanted to do. It felt really terrible for the students and some of the staff. So, we thought that we needed student events on campus.

Although Kelsey was only a first-year teacher, she organized a school prom that was a success, and school leaders acknowledged this work by raising her salary. During her two years at the school, she "planned the first-ever prom, the first-ever talent show, bake sales, winter carnival . . . whatever traditional schools do, we did. That was an epic undertaking—with the budgeting, fund-raising, and doing all those things."

Despite the raise, Kelsey did not get a sense that the administration understood how much energy and time she spent on these extracurricular activities. Nor did they advise her to limit her activities or encourage others to work with her so that the duties would be spread around. (When she decided to leave the school, Kelsey had to reach out to four teachers to divide the responsibilities for the student activities she had been implementing.) She and her colleagues eventually learned to be cautious about raising concerns, making suggestions, or volunteering. "We kind of got to this place where last year people weren't going to propose things because they weren't going to carry them. So, I would only speak up when it was something I wanted to carry, something I felt that needed to be carried or done."

In addition to organizing the extracurricular activities, Kelsey decided to see if she could make some changes within the school day for students who were doing well and on the honor roll. Concluding that the school focused most of its energy on students who were failing or acting out, she decided that there needed to be recognition for the students who had begun to do well as soon as they entered the charter school.

> I started an Academic Congress which brings students together; the honor roll students once a quarter go on some educational trip around Boston. Then I created an award for the students that had the best attendance, earned the least number of demerits, and had the highest GPA. I kind of calculated all of this in a formula, and they would get their name on a plaque in the hall.

Kelsey did all of this in addition to teaching an extended day: she left home by 7:30 a.m. and got home at 6 p.m. Her students recognized that she worked incredibly hard as a teacher. She was able to challenge them academically *and* relate to them as individuals. At the school's senior banquet, one student stood up and said, "I hated history until I got to [Kelsey's] class."

Kelsey received some mentoring and support from outside her school when she joined the Consortium for Excellence in Teacher Education

(CETE) group of Boston-area urban teachers from regular and charter schools that met five times a year. As the facilitator of the group, I was able to offer some advice as well as a sympathetic ear. Kelsey is a good storyteller who was able to laugh when she recounted the challenges she was facing in and outside of the classroom. Despite the perspective and support she received from this group, Kelsey's dedication to teaching and improving the culture of the school took "a huge personal toll." After two years of this intense work, she decided to move back to Vermont with her boyfriend. "I graduated college in three years. I'm pretty motivated, pretty on my game. But I don't think I ever expected it to consume my life. [Finishing college in three years] was easy. This school has consumed my life for the last two years . . . the stress was incredible."

Kelsey's life might have felt less stressful if her administrators had expressed their appreciation for her contributions instead of criticizing her for speaking up. That message has also been received by her colleagues, as Kelsey notes:

> We've talked a lot about who is going to speak up. And there's no clear answer to that, because there are a lot of people in the department who feel that there's going to be some kind of negative repercussion if they do, because the school is so small . . . You shouldn't feel like things are not going well in your classroom, and it could be a real easy fix, but you can't say anything. I definitely have colleagues that feel that they can't say anything.

As noted in the previous chapter, first- or second-year teachers in charter schools, especially those who have not had the advantage of much preparation or mentoring, are still very much in the process of learning how to be effective teachers. When these beginning teachers who appear to have leadership potential are expected to assume extra responsibilities, they may be flattered and excited about the opportunity. They are willing to lead, but do not have much knowledge or skills about how to make effective change. Moreover, unlike Grace and Lee, who were experienced teachers and who had received mentoring in their school, these eager young people usually do not get much advice about how to proceed, especially in schools where administrators may perceive questions about the school's functioning as challenges to their authority.

As we read in Kelsey's story, it can be overwhelming for beginning teachers to take on too many responsibilities during their first couple of years, when they are still learning how to teach. Many of these dedicated young people burn out and leave sooner or later, depending on the kind of support they receive and their fit with the culture of their school. While there are many other people eager to apply to a vacancy in a charter school, a model that is built on such turnover wastes the skills, support, and wisdom that experienced teachers could offer to beginning teachers interested in effecting institutional as well as instructional change.

Kelsey decided to leave this charter school at the end of her second year. While one can argue that she might have moved on in any case, there is also the possibility that, given appropriate mentoring and advice, her path might have been different. With guidance, for instance, she could have learned to limit the number of school initiatives to undertake during her first years of teaching. Perhaps she would not have felt so totally consumed by her work at school. Nor would she have felt unappreciated. "I think that it's nice, when you're doing 150 percent as a first- or second-year teacher, to have someone say [they] notice ... Maybe some of that recognition will come when I leave, but that's too late."

» LAURA
Finding Mentors to Support Leadership Development

The next story about institutional teacher leadership also takes place in a mission-driven small urban school in the Boston area. Laura was a second-stage teacher when a mentor, arranged through the Brandeis/CETE induction program, helped her undertake and analyze a teacher action research project. The combination of a mentor able to work with her in school and the CETE group of supportive colleagues helped Laura persist as she worked with teachers and parents.

Laura, a lovely, thoughtful, and centered young woman who grew up in a sophisticated family concerned about social justice inside and outside of the United States, attended Dartmouth as an undergraduate. She began her teaching career as an NYC Teaching Fellow. Her only teacher education preparation was a six-week preservice program where she cotaught middle school summer school with the teacher who had failed the students in the first place. Laura described this introduction to teaching as a "complete nightmare." Thus she was pleased to get emotional support from a woman teacher in her department assigned to mentor her during her first year, when, as one of sixty-five English teachers working with 5,000 students in a New York City high school, she was struggling to learn how to teach and to control her large classes. Laura reports that "this mentor relationship turned out to be very important for moral support and helping me get though tough emotional stress, but it really wasn't about instruction."

It was not until her second year that Laura, assigned to teach an Advanced Placement English class, found Kevin, a colleague who helped her to articulate teaching goals and gain a repertoire of instructional strategies appropriate for her classes:

> I was working closely with Kevin, who had been teaching Advanced Placement. He probably had been teaching for seven or eight years. I still think he might be the best teacher I ever encountered, at least as a colleague. He was incredible, and we did everything together. We did all our lesson planning together; we graded each other's student work and sort of graded anchor papers together and used rubrics . . . He was the only colleague I had who was consuming research on his own and sharing it with me . . . Really, that was my only experience of collaborative teaching.

Kevin played a crucial role in helping her develop professionally as an English teacher. As a result, Laura was introduced to the idea that a mentor could be an important partner as she explored ideas about teaching and learning.

After two years of teaching five sections of English classes with thirty-four students in each class in that large urban high school, Laura had had enough. She moved to Boston, where she substituted for a couple of years, eventually becoming a teacher in a Boston Public Pilot high school. (Boston Pilot schools are small innovative schools that are part of the Boston Public Schools and follow the teachers' contract. Educators in the twenty-one Boston Pilot schools, which enroll approximately 9,000 students, receive training and support from the nonprofit Center for Collaborative Education.) In the small urban school of approximately 200 students that Laura joined as a teacher, she was relieved to find that her largest class was composed of twenty-two students.

> I much preferred the smaller setting, for all the reasons research doesn't necessarily support. I just felt I could know my students so much better, really spend time giving quality feedback, as opposed to just speeding through hundreds of papers . . . You know, when it gets around in a small school that a teacher is working hard for kids, they know that, and they kind of come together and have their own ways of showing they appreciate it . . . It really helped classroom management [to not be] an issue.

It is not a coincidence that Grace, Lee, Kelsey, and Laura developed good relationships with their students. Many educators who assume some kind of institutional leadership are teachers like Grace, who ask: "What makes kids want to be here? How can I make school a more successful place for kids?"

Two things changed for Laura in her fifth year of teaching. First, she joined the monthly meetings of the Brandeis/CETE group, where she found urban and suburban teachers who were reflecting about their teaching. Her motivation for joining this group was "to network with other teachers and learn more about the qualities people shared that brought them to this work and kept them in the work." Second, in 2008, the Brandeis/CETE group invited second-stage teachers to submit proposals for action research projects that would address some pedagogical or institutional problem they were experiencing.

Laura submitted a proposal "because I thought I could have an active learning experience while contributing something to my community . . . I felt like this could be a motivation for me to take what I was reading and thinking about and share it with my school community."

She decided to work with her Advanced Placement English class to research how communication between educators at the school and parents could be improved. Laura envisioned this work as demonstrating to her class (which was studying rhetoric) how the kind of rhetoric the teachers and school administrators were using to communicate with parents could be more persuasive. She was also pleased to learn that, due to funds from the Arthur Vining Davis Foundation, the Brandeis/CETE program would be able to assign Matt, a Boston College doctoral student mentor, to work with her on the action research project. For her, this meant she could recreate the power of good mentoring that she had experienced in New York.

Originally envisioned as a classroom extension of learning about rhetoric that focused on parent communications in two grades, this action research project soon grew more complicated and demanding when Laura's headmaster urged her to survey all parents in grades six through twelve—a much larger research program that involved gathering large quantities of data. As the scope of the project grew and became very demanding of their time, Laura and her students found themselves meeting regularly after school.

In addition, the headmaster wanted Laura to coordinate this survey with the work of a standing committee of parents and a counselor that had been tasked with examining school/parent communications. Although he was trying to have Laura's work become an intrinsic part of that year's goals for the school, the headmaster's request actually made her work more political and time consuming. Not only did this request further increase the scope of the task, it also meant that Laura needed to spend time working with a committee, which required that she use listening, advocating, and negotiating skills.

While the headmaster was supportive of teacher leadership and encouraged this initiative, Laura did not have a clear idea about who had the authority to implement ideas. Was it the committee? Should she proceed independently and report to the headmaster? She reported that "it was confusing . . . like trying to take authority when it was never publically handed to you." The headmaster had complicated the original task by urging her to survey the entire school instead of just the parents in her two classes; he also wanted her to coordinate her work with a standing committee, a task that required time and patience. She did not feel as though she could refuse either of these requests.

(While it may be challenging for any teacher to refuse a request from a principal, it seems that women have more difficulty turning down a request, especially from a supervisor. Henning and Jardin, who founded the Simmons School of Management, an MBA program designed exclusively for women, often warned that women take on too much responsibility for the work that needs to be done, rather than thinking about their career paths as many men have been trained to do.[2] Women also find it difficult to say no.[3] Women educators who want to become leaders may need to be supported as they learn to be selective about which tasks they agree to assume.)

Matt, Laura's mentor from Boston College, played a critical role throughout the process. Working inside the school, he helped Laura and her students develop and articulate their research focus, create a survey, and process the data. While she and her students were wary about changing the scope of her research, Matt urged them "not to get discouraged, because this actually meant that if we found something of statistical significance it would potentially mean more." He helped her think about how to navigate relationships with her peers, the committee of parents and counselor, and the headmaster. At the end of the semester, the mentor also helped Laura and her students learn how "to present the data to the instructional leadership team in a way that they might be most receptive . . . He helped me think about how to do both—serve the bigger school community through the research while making it a valuable learning experience for my students." Matt was a sounding board for Laura as she was learning how to operate within the formal and informal power relationships in the school.

Researchers have recently been focusing on the importance of strengthening social capital when teachers, parents, and administrators work together. Hargreaves and Fullan write: "Social capital refers to how the quantity and quality of interactions and social relations among people affects their access to knowledge and information; their senses of expectation, obligation, and trust; and how far they are likely to adhere to the same norms or codes of behavior."[4] In this case, Matt gave Laura a safe place to share her frustration and to reflect on next steps. Instead of giving up on her action research project when she was urged to enlarge its scope and pressured to spend time working with a standing committee, Laura—with the help of her mentor—was able to learn much more about how social capital and relational trust operated in her Pilot school. Her increased understanding was important to keep the momentum of her project going.

> I learned a lot; my students learned a lot. I think ultimately the Instructional Leadership Team learned a lot that they didn't know ... parents were yearning for a lot more outreach ... they didn't feel invited to be part of the process of helping their kids through school ... And I was really pleased by the fact that my students could be the messengers with statistical evidence to show that this is how our parents felt.

Laura was able to achieve her objectives for her action plan, although she was disappointed that the outreach initiative to parents was not fully institutionalized when she left that school at the end of the year to enter a doctoral program. She reflected that the mentoring and action research "really made it more bittersweet for me to leave, because I felt like it positioned me in my last year to do the best work I had done in the classroom and got me thinking about the parents of my own students." In fact, her action research, which focused on improving communications with parents, had the unintended result of helping her and the students realize that not only did parents feel shut out of decision making, but students also felt that they were rarely asked for their opinions about what was working well or otherwise in the school.

> I could have really tried to build on it if I was still there, just trying to involve the students in the same way we were trying to involve the parents in the school ... I mean the structure of the school is such that the teachers basically make all the policy decisions and decisions about how to implement policy, and the students, really a lot of them, resent the fact that they're not asked for input.

As Laura moved on, she acknowledged that her experience of teacher leadership in the arena of institutional culture and governance could have been more successful if it had been more than a one-year initiative. However, she noted how valuable the experience had been. "I feel that if I become a principal or superintendent later, I have personal knowledge of things that actually work. I would encourage my teachers to engage in this type of work and create an environment that incentivizes teachers to do that."

As an outside mentor, Matt played a key role in helping Laura and her students implement an action research project that enlarged her vision and understanding of what was possible:

+ Increasing parental communication and expanding the school's perceptions about parents' and students' potential contributions;
+ Increasing the teachers' and students' voice and agency;
+ Involving students in an experiential and relevant learning project. (The students will not soon forget what they learned about rhetoric.)

It is fair to conclude that Laura would not have been able to complete this research project satisfactorily without Matt's support. On a less positive note, the Brandeis/CETE project was unable to continue offering mentors for urban teacher action research projects when the grant funding ended, although the group is continuing to meet for monthly dinner meetings supported by participant contributions.

REFLECTIONS

The teacher leaders described in this chapter found their own voices while speaking out of personal concern about their students and/or their colleagues. They had no official leadership roles, although they earned credibility and trust as strong teachers and people of integrity. Informal teacher leadership does not always have a continuing institutional impact on the school's structure or authority, partly because it *is* informal and outside the regular channels of power.

Educators often move into the arena of institutional leadership because of their frustration with the institutional constraints and politics that they think are negatively impacting their ability to be effective teachers. When Kelsey became concerned that disciplinary interactions in school among young people and adults were having a negative effect on learning, she decided to organize some extracurricular activities that would create more trusting relationships within the school. Lee, on the other hand, became involved because she was tired of hearing the misunderstandings and negative speculation among teachers about the principals. When she took the initiative to create better communication, she helped improve the school's culture. Whatever the motivation, when teachers begin to become involved in issues outside of their classrooms, they may discover that they have an interest and affinity for seeing the bigger picture. The New Teachers Project at the Harvard Graduate School of Education has noted that incoming teachers have different and higher expectations than previous generations of teachers about how they should be treated; they anticipate a less hierarchical school culture and better working conditions.[5] Those who are graduates of liberal arts colleges and universities often have self-confidence and a sense of agency and mission. They are more interested in becoming what Charles Taylor Kerchner describes as "owners of their work and self-managers."[6] Many of those who enter the field of teaching today because of social justice concerns are eager to work collegially to make changes in how schools function.

Challenges often arise when teachers begin to act as leaders or question how the school functions. Reena Freedman, the induction coordinator at Gann Academy, a pluralist Jewish day high school in Waltham, Massachusetts, notes that teachers need to become institutionally competent as well as culturally competent. As the four institutional teacher leaders described in this chapter found, they needed to learn how the school as a whole functioned and how their initiatives would fit in. Each learned the importance of leadership, culture, and organization in the schools in which they were working. Because none of these informal teacher leaders was enrolled in an administrative program where she would learn about organizational, political, and human resources analyses and skills, the kind of mentoring they each received had a very important impact on their success and/or frustration.

The situation in small urban schools focused on an urgent mission to improve student achievement is particularly complex. As with suburban public schools, there are significant differences among urban charter schools and small alternative schools. Some function democratically and encourage teachers' voices; others have a single point of authority that is usually more rigid and hierarchical. One would think that mission-driven charter and alternative schools would welcome teacher leadership, since there is so much work to be done. Some teachers who are eager to contribute ideas and suggestions, however, have found that taking initiative or having divergent ideas was not appreciated by administrators in some charter schools, especially those with more of a top-down hierarchical structure. For example, Kelsey felt neither supported nor appreciated by administrators when she raised concerns on behalf of her colleagues. She left the school after two of the most stressful years she had ever experienced. On the other hand, Laura's story about her work in a Boston Pilot school where the principal was very committed to supporting teacher leadership is much more positive. Laura received support from an outside mentor (funded by a CETE grant from the Arthur Vining Davis Foundation) who was able to help her navigate challenges presented by colleagues and administrators. Kelsey and Laura, two similar young educators with intelligence, energy, and passion about improving urban education, had stories with quite different outcomes.

Why did institutional leadership initiatives work in some of these secondary school settings but not in others? Here are some conclusions I think we can draw from these stories. First, just as it takes time to learn how to be an effective teacher, it takes time and knowledge about how the school works to become an effective institutional teacher leader. It makes sense that the teacher leaders in the suburban school and the Boston Pilot school were second-stage teachers who had had time to develop the political skills for undertaking an initiative, including ways to involve and work with administrators. In contrast, although Kelsey was very successful in creating a range of positive activities for the students in her school, she could not possibly maintain all of the student activities and the faculty advocacy that she began as a first-year teacher. Moreover, she was left alone to take on the administrators and did not know how to find allies within the school who would stand with her publicly.

Second, relationships among the adults are key to effective institutional leadership. Grace and Lee learned how to navigate and make connections based on relationships that went beyond departmental collegiality and boundaries. Informal institutional teacher leaders are often women who have been excluded from power in schools for so long that they become very skilled in maneuvering through relationships. Thus, both Grace and Lee perceived that much of leadership is relationship based, and they worked to find who was playing which role and how to develop ways to work with people they did not know. Laura's mentor helped her negotiate social capital issues in her school; she learned that part of her project's success depended on reaching out to existing groups at the school. These teacher leaders had to gain skills for reading the institutional landscape in order to help their projects succeed. As Casey, the instructional teacher leader we met in the last chapter, notes:

> I think what makes things successful is when I'm able to articulate what's about to happen, versus trying to create something that nobody really wants to do. Things are successful when everybody was almost about to do it anyway. I like paying attention to other people and seeing what people are already about to do; it fits my personality type.

Third, mentors can also be incredibly helpful in developing and supporting institutional leaders. An inside or outside mentor can provide much-needed help to teachers who want to learn how to create attainable goals, navigate among those who have power in a school, build support, and anticipate opposition. Laura's mentor helped her and her students figure out how to deal with the pressure they were under in having to expand the number of surveys in their communications project—as it became a schoolwide teacher research project. He helped them to "roll with the punches."

Fourth, being an institutional leader requires a great amount of energy and dedication, because it comes on top of the very real demands involved in being an excellent teacher. It helps if educators who want to improve the school are motivated by a passion or vision that will energize and sustain them as they work to make the vision a reality. Since much of Grace's work (including her four years advising the Step Squad) was fueled by her passion for equity, she recognized that she could use a crisis about race to strengthen diversity and justice in the school culture.

Fifth, there are a variety of roles available to those who want to be institutional teacher leaders. There is often room to create a role that matches the style and strengths of each teacher interested in such leadership. Lee found herself in different roles: at one time reaching out to the Latino community, and at other times being a respected messenger who could clear up lingering misunderstandings and rumors. Such informal institutional initiatives also enable teachers to move into and out of engagement, depending on what is happening in their lives outside of school.

Sixth, most secondary school institutional leadership is informal and associated with the teacher/s who take the leadership. The informal nature of secondary school teacher leadership, however, often means that few of these initiatives are institutionalized when the teacher leader moves on to another issue or leaves the school, unless the teacher and/or administrator make a specific effort to do so. Thus, Laura's initiative ended when she left the school. It is possible that the project could have been institutionalized if it had continued for two or more years.

Finally, it makes a difference if the school's administrative leaders have established a school culture and organization that is supportive of teachers raising questions, making suggestions, and taking initiative. It may seem that all schools would welcome teacher leadership, but as we have seen, that is not true. As we will read in the next chapter, there must be support inside and/or outside for these teacher leaders as they encounter resistance, take on tasks that may grow to be unmanageable, or reflect on whether they want to be performing these teacher leader roles.

It's a norm that administrators don't trust teachers, and teachers don't trust administrators. How can we educate our children, challenge them to take risks, if we, the adults in the community, don't trust each other?

—Monique, principal of a New York City small school

4 SUPPORTING TEACHER LEADERSHIP

The Role of Principals

ASPIRING TEACHER LEADERS often express frustration about the lack of support they receive in their schools. Some eventually give up on any efforts to improve their schools because of what they perceive as the lack of leadership, power struggles, or inconsistent goals and communication in their schools. In my work with teacher leaders, I heard too many stories about the obstacles teachers felt prevented them from being effective. As a former principal and school superintendent, I could not understand why or how administrators would not support these bright and dedicated teachers who want to improve their schools. What I learned through my research with teacher leaders and principals was that the picture was more complicated than I had expected. Some of the questions that arose were: Why isn't it easy for a principal to put into practice what she may support theoretically? What kind of challenges is a principal likely to encounter even if he does support the idea of teacher leadership? How can principals learn from each other's successes and problems in the arena of teacher leadership?

My conversations with teacher leaders—as discussed in previous chapters—indicated that support from administrators plays a crucial role in developing both instructional and institutional teacher leadership. As we will read in this chapter, administrators who decide that it is in their (and their school's) interest to develop teacher leaders need to take steps so that everyone understands why and how the culture and organization of the school are changing.

When analyzing the interactions between principals and teacher leaders, it is important to understand the larger framework in which principals operate. As a result of cumulative expectations, principals are faced with too many responsibilities for one person, including:

+ *Instructional:* Establishing a vision for the school; framing short- and long-term goals; overseeing curriculum, instruction, and assessment;
+ *Institutional:* Budgeting (including fund-raising in the case of a charter school); implementing policy; supervising day-to-day functioning (including but not limited to scheduling, buses, discipline, meals, testing, Americans with Disabilities Act [ADA] compliance, and fire drills);
+ *Students and community:* Modeling how adults should address student needs in a challenging, fair, and supportive culture; affirming diversity; implementing discipline; interacting with parents and guardians;
+ *Human resources:* Hiring a team of diverse and talented faculty and staff members; administering professional development; negotiating with union representatives; supervising and evaluating faculty and staff members;
+ *Political:* Directing the allocation of limited resources; overseeing communications and outreach inside and outside the school, including the community at large;
+ *Symbolic:* Being a voice for students and adults who may not be heard, and celebrating their accomplishments.

Since this is not by any means a complete list of the tasks school leaders are expected to undertake, principals cannot possibly accomplish all of these responsibilities by themselves. It would appear that they have much to gain from working with teacher leaders to strengthen the school's institutional culture and teaching and learning.

Yet even if mobilizing teacher leaders might be a good way to share some instructional tasks, distributing leadership among teachers is not as simple as it might seem. One reason for this is that the perception of teachers and the roles they play has become part of a larger dialogue about how to reform schools. On the one hand, entrepreneurial reformers and media experts are proclaiming that teachers bear total responsibility for whether students have or have not been able to achieve. They advocate the recruiting of young people who have been excellent students to teach for a couple of years, even if they do not know much about teaching. They recommend using prescribed curricula and instructional methods so that there will be uniformity in how content is taught, and that it be closely monitored by frequent testing to assess whether the students have learned the material. These advocates want to implement a "business model" that focuses on accountability by firing those teachers whose performance is in the bottom 10 percent, removing the due process provisions of tenure, and eliminating seniority as a means of assigning teachers. They also think that teachers should compete for merit pay, challenging longstanding district/union contracts that award teachers raises for graduate degrees and more years of teaching. In such a scenario, most principals focus on standards, student and teacher assessment, and teacher evaluation.

Many educators, however, do not believe that these proposed changes are going to improve teaching and learning. They have seen reforms come and go without having had an impact on what Larry Cuban calls the "black box" of classroom practice.[1] Of course, administrators would like it to be easier to select their teachers, pay them higher salaries, and remove ineffective teachers. Because they recognize how challenging it is to change the contractual agreement that governs the district, however, these experienced principals prefer to focus on the school arenas where they have power to improve instruction. They decide to build and maintain a collaborative culture where teachers can work together to address significant instructional and institutional challenges. These administrators recognize that they are dependent on their teachers to change the pedagogy and curriculum as needed, and they look to teachers to take leadership in these areas.

Hargreaves and Fullan, who write about the importance of social and professional capital, where educators can learn from each other, believe that high-quality peer collaboration depends upon:

+ The conditions that allow for professionals to meet (high performing countries provide more time for this than do low performers);

+ Expectations and frameworks of learning and curriculum that are challenging and open enough for teachers to innovate and inquire into their practice together (i.e., to have something significant to meet about);

+ Ongoing timely data that enable teachers, individually and together, to diagnose student learning needs and coordinate their instructional responses;

+ Outstanding, stable leadership that can galvanize professionals as a team in pursuit of a greater good (rather than principals or political leaders who come and go through revolving doors of school leadership);

+ Opportunities, as well as incentives, to learn from colleagues in other classrooms, other schools, and even other countries (as in Singapore, for instance) in the quest for ever higher performance.[2]

The question for principals is how to establish these conditions. How can groups or teams of teachers learn from each other about how to expand the capacities of all students, including those with poor attendance, those who are English language learners, and those with disabilities? How can a school become a professional learning community with a culture that supports strong teacher leaders as well as those educators who are struggling? We have seen that teacher leaders become involved in school reform for many reasons, including a desire to create a more positive institutional climate for students and teachers. Some educators become energized by thinking about the larger picture of how a school functions. They are willing to advise students in an extracurricular activity or do outreach to unrepresented students and parents. They often serve on committees, make suggestions, and volunteer after school hours.

We would expect that all principals would welcome this thoughtful and free additional labor offered by some of the leading educators in the school. Yet it is not the case that teacher leaders are always welcomed in schools. Some principals have a top-down hierarchical vision of how schools should operate and do not want to share power with teachers. Others feel they have their hands full working to develop a coherent administrative team, and that is all that they can handle. Nor is anyone holding principals accountable for how effectively they support teacher leadership.

If the school intends to educate young people to make critical choices, principals need to understand that they also must create and maintain a professional culture based on selecting, supporting, and trusting teachers who make thoughtful, reflective decisions. As Bryk and Schneider describe,[3] this is not a laissez-faire trust where educators are left to do their own thing without any kind of accountability. Rather, it is trust that is earned as hard-working colleagues discuss together how to improve teaching and learning. Their goals are not only to understand the interests and strengths of the young people they are teaching, but also to learn from diagnostic assessments, research, and each other how best to anticipate instructional problems and help their classes achieve learning goals. (I would also point out that conversations in which educators share their vulnerabilities and take some academic risks do not flourish in a "gotcha" climate where principals are mandated to document teachers' struggles and less than successful attempts.)

Principals face their own challenges as they balance how to create a collegial culture with the demand to ensure that teachers are effective. Most principals recognize that they don't have a monopoly on ideas about how to improve schools, and they know that they are actually dependent on the teachers who will implement the reforms in their classrooms. Therefore, they should welcome the idea of teacher involvement in instructional decisions because of (1) teachers' vision and understanding of how schools need to change, and (2) teachers' experiences in how schools function when they work well. At the same time, principals are the school-based leaders who must decide which teachers will continue to teach and which will be asked to leave. Many principals are thus much more cautious about sharing power with teachers in the arenas of personnel, budgeting, and politics, which are perceived as the administrator's domain.

This chapter will explain why school leaders (and teachers) need to evolve and articulate a more complex understanding of the principal's relationships with the teachers, students, and parents who make up the school community.

» MONIQUE
Building a Democratic School with Shared Instructional Leadership

Monique is a strong and visionary African American principal who gathered a group of young teachers to create a small New York City urban high school—The Nelson Mandela School for Social Democracy. This mission-driven NYC school was founded on the recognition that students need to prepare to become citizens in a democracy while they are also becoming academically successful students who can pass the New York State Regents exams and some performance assessments. An Insideschools review notes:

> [The Nelson Mandela School for Social Democracy] is committed to offering its students, many of whom are alienated and poorly prepared for high school, a strong liberal arts education with lots of individual attention, an emphasis on moral values, and a sense of community. The school, opened in 2005 in the Park West High School complex, has an idealistic, close-knit faculty, a coherent philosophy, and a clear sense of mission. Founded with the support of a Boston-based not-for-profit organization, ... the school encourages students to look at events in history as a basis for making decisions in their own lives. They may study the origins of the Holocaust, for example, and examine how various participants abetted the slaughter or acted against it. The students identify "bystanders," "perpetrators," "victims," and "upstanders" (people who resist the perpetrators) ... The hope is for students to see themselves as actors rather than passive

observers in events as small as the bullying of a fellow student or as a large as the waging of a war overseas.[4]

The Mandela School for Social Democracy is also a part of the New York Performance Standards Consortium, a coalition of successful small schools that have developed alternatives to standardized tests.

Monique, the founding principal of the school, states: "I believe that I am all that New York City schools are—good and bad. I came from Trinidad, and I started school in [Bedford Stuyvesant]. I was teased because of my accent and hair. I complained and no one listened." Although she believed that "school was a place that was supposed to give me a ladder and a language to a world that I was curious about," she found her large secondary schools boring and sterile. She eventually overcame her boredom when she attended a small school where she felt that the teachers knew her as a person.

When Monique became a teacher, she "saw the other side of the dance. People said 'do and move.' Do the curriculum and move the students." Because she had experienced that as a student, she was excited to find colleagues with a different vision about preparing students to become citizens in our democracy when she attended Facing History and Ourselves workshops. These workshops confirmed her belief that "teachers needed support to be able to create classes that not only engage their students, but that they find engaging." She decided to help create a small NYC high school that would focus on students becoming "citizens who choose to contribute." As Michael, one teacher at the school observes: "Part of it is which skills we think students will need to be successful here and in college or in real work. The ability to follow directions is a skill that people need, but so is the ability to question directions and advocate for yourself. For us, being a successful student means you can do both of those things."

In this school, the concept of a learning community applies to adults as well as students. Because the new principal had previously worked in a school that affirmed teacher leadership, she decided to build the concept of teacher leadership into the application for a new small school. But Monique knew it would take more than words in the application to the New York City Department of Education for a new small high school to make teacher leadership a reality. She notes that "it's a norm that administrators don't trust teachers, and teachers don't trust administrators. How can we educate our children, challenge them to take risks, if we, the adults in the community, don't trust each other?" Before the beginning of the school's third year, she decided to allocate time and money to send two faculty groups to the National School Reform Facility's (NSRF) training program for facilitative leadership. She told the teachers that she would select one team of teachers, and they would choose the other. In addition to demonstrating transparency in the selection process, Monique was acknowledging that she and the teachers might select different people for this training. Demonstrating trust in her faculty members also guaranteed that there would be greater ownership in terms of obtained results.

Between the two teams, almost one third of the teachers learned new skills and increased self-confidence by participating in these workshops. Michael is a thoughtful young teacher who was a member of the Ultimate Frisbee team and earned his teaching certification as an undergraduate at Brandeis University. He is passionate about his work in this inner city school. He joined the school in its second year and was selected by his peers to participate in the NSRF training, which enabled him to learn strategies for leading small groups of teachers looking at student work, discussing classroom dilemmas as part of a Critical Friends Group, developing support strategies for students, and organizing and facilitating effective meetings. As more teachers began to take responsibility and initiative in mentoring beginning teachers, raising questions about how the school operates, and thinking about the culture of the school.

The results of this training could be observed each fall when the teachers ran staff development sessions for new teachers. Michael notes: "When new teachers show up at our school in August, they see teachers running the school. The principal and assistant principal were always there, but they weren't the ones running every single aspect." Charles Kerchner notes that there is a different division of labor in a small school where teachers share responsibility for running the school: "Adult roles are more diverse and much less specialized. There are relatively more teachers engaged in the core academic subjects and fewer ancillary personnel. There are more shared responsibilities."⁵ At this school, experienced teachers encourage each other to take on additional school responsibilities such as identifying topics for professional development.

Monique, who worked even harder than the teachers, was an inspiring role model who encouraged Michael and others to become leaders who could contribute even more to their students and school. Unlike teachers who cherish their instructional autonomy in suburban and other more traditional schools, teachers in this small urban high school were willing to speak with their colleagues on what they observe in classrooms. This reflected the culture of the school, where learning about a "universe of obligations" means that it is essential to become responsible for others. Monique said: "In our mission statement we say that we want them to become citizens who choose to participate. And we tell them over and over that that's a choice, but it's also a responsibility." She wanted to work with teachers who made the same choice to assume responsibilities.

Monique provided mentoring so that Michael and other teachers could develop positive ways to interact with colleagues. When he did peer observations (which are not used in formal evaluations written up by administrators), Michael was very much aware that he was a peer and not an administrator who has power over his peers. He knew that he must be careful not to "overstep" in his interactions with his peers:

> Today I was working with one student, and the teacher and another student were sort of getting into it. And I didn't see it as my role to step in, because that would be violating both the relationship [and] also the authority of that teacher. So, I'll step in if I'm not overstepping my relationship.

While Michael believes that the skills he learned at the NSRF training session were very valuable, he concluded that his effectiveness as a teacher leader depends more on relationships he has been able to develop than on specific skills or rubrics learned at a workshop. And one of those key relationships was with his principal. When asked what kind of support he got from Monique, he answered "unwavering."

It was listening when I was just at wit's end about not being able to do all of the work . . . The support came in listening, in putting me in situations where, at the moment, I didn't have the skills to be successful in them, but she supported me through check-ins, in talking through agendas for meetings, in encouraging and inviting me to participate in leadership training, reaching out to all of her staff. We all have her cell phone number. We can call her whenever we want. Really, I think that the support came in believing in my potential and setting me up in situations that would maximize that potential, but also recognizing that I needed help, and creating the space where she could provide that help.

Monique mentored Michael by pushing him into situations where he was challenged and helping him grow through training and by making herself accessible for advice.

Monique pushed the teachers to take some risks and was there to support them when they struggled. She recognized the developmental needs of her faculty. She also knew that when a school asks for 150 percent every day from a teacher, there will be times when it is important to support teachers by letting them spend some time away from the school to deal with their personal or professional needs. Not surprisingly, her school was able to develop a very loyal, hard-working, and passionate core of teachers.

As a result of Monique's commitment to transparent decision making, decisions about who took on which tasks were not perceived to be based solely on the principal's preferences. Teachers can become immobilized when the basis for a principal's decisions appears arbitrary, but Monique's approach not only helped teachers understand how and why the decisions were made, but also empowered those who cared to participate in the process.

One of the challenges that principals of small alternative and charter schools face is high teacher turnover. Because of the schools' very long working hours and the institutional intensity, even teachers who love working in such a passionate environment can become worn out and decide to leave. Recognizing this, Monique encouraged her faculty members when they wanted to undertake professional development. She supported Michael, who had spent four years as a teacher and teacher leader, when he wanted to enroll in a part-time master's leadership program at Bank Street College. Michael eventually decided that he could not continue to be a full-time teacher at the Mandela School for Social Democracy, even though he wanted to remain at the school. As he considered his options, he realized that:

> I don't think I could go back to being "just a classroom teacher," where I close my door, I teach my class, I go home. I don't think I could teach in a school where that type of teacher existed. So, if I remain a classroom teacher, I see it being in this type of environment, even though I don't know how to survive as a teacher in this environment long term.

Michael was only one of the teachers mentored by this principal. Because Monique institutionalized teacher leadership at the core of the school, faculty members understood from the beginning that there was a shared expectation to contribute inside and outside the classroom. She also helped them gain skills to become competent in these additional responsibilities. Michael notes that even after Monique was promoted and left, the school's organization continued to be "based on the premise that teachers have an integral stake in and responsibility to participate in the direction of the school, that teachers are involved in the school just as they are in their own classrooms . . . Teacher leadership means that teachers take on helping to shape the direction of the school."

After she left, however, there was major turnover of administrators and teachers, and the school encountered challenges to carrying on what this visionary principal had introduced, because the new administrators were trying to support so many beginning teachers.

Monique was a principal of a small urban school. When we next examine the principal's leadership in a large suburban secondary school, we will observe that, although some of the principles about the interactions between administrators and teacher leaders are the same, the implementation is quite different. The organization and culture found in a large high school require different approaches and strategies.

» SAMANTHA

Going from Good to Great in a Large Suburban School

Just as Monique had been, Samantha, the new principal of a large high school in the Boston suburbs, was deeply committed to developing and supporting teacher leadership both instructionally and institutionally. She remembers her own experiences as a teacher with frustration. When she had tried to demonstrate leadership as a teacher, she felt that she "was thwarted in every area. The principal screamed, yelled, and told me to go back to my place." (One of the great pleasures of her career was to meet him again after she had been named a principal.) She was excited, then, when she was appointed principal at Northern High, a school with a long tradition of teacher autonomy and support for teacher voices.

"Sam" believed that it was her responsibility to create the overall direction and vision for the school. The size of this large school created structural dilemmas for the principal as well as for teachers who wanted to demonstrate leadership. She concluded that changing the school's instructional climate and culture would be necessary if the school were to advance from being very good to great. She therefore appointed Joan (whom we met in chapter 1), a respected English teacher in her eighth year of teaching at the school, to be vice principal and to lead the school's initiative to create Critical Friends Groups, where teachers could reflect together on their work.

Sam knew that she didn't (and couldn't) have all the answers for moving such a large and complicated institution forward. She did understand that "once the vision is clear, teachers often have the best idea of how to go in that direction." One of the challenges she faced was how to hear the voices of teachers, since "in a large school, exerting school-level leadership is a scary thing . . . Speaking in front of the entire faculty is intimidating." And because of the size and complexity of this school, Sam understood that she could not be the key person working directly with teachers.

The principal of a large secondary school is often seen as distant from day-to-day teaching and learning. Much of his or her work focuses on leadership and administration from a perspective that is a mile up:

working with others to craft a schoolwide vision; developing and assessing year-long school goals; creating a budget; serving as liaison between the school and the central office and between the school and the community; coping with day-to-day student and adult crises; and managing the impact of construction projects on the school. Interviews with teacher leaders working in this school affirmed that few of them understood that (or how) their principal supports teacher leadership. This is partly because the primary interactions of the principal of a large middle or high school are with department chairs, who become the liaisons between teachers and the principal. Principals also may not understand that they are perceived as distant from day-to-day instruction.

Although Sam would not be working directly with the teachers, her own experience as an innovative teacher enabled her to understand that teacher leaders need certain skills in order to be effective:

+ The ability to think structurally and organizationally about what can be accomplished;
+ "The understanding that your reality is not the same as everyone else's, which means that you should not be judgmental about your peers";
+ Adaptability and flexibility ("your original idea may be modified multiple times");
+ The ability to take advantage of leadership opportunities.

She decided that it was her responsibility to provide training and mentoring in the school so that teachers would be able to attain these skills. She also thought that she should provide needed resources: "I'm the resource person. You tell me what you need, I'll find the resources."

One of the resources she offered was focus and support from Joan, whose primary responsibility was to support change and leadership. Sam and Joan made a good team. Working with department chairs and teacher leaders, they focused on several initiatives: (1) narrowing the achievement gap at this affluent and diverse suburban high school; (2) establishing a peer tutoring group; (3) consistently implementing school rules, such as the consequences for poor attendance in class; (4) creating a teacher training program based in the high school; and (5) supporting a network of teacher leaders who convene groups of teachers to examine curriculum, instruction, and assessment, and thus improve the culture of the school. Both were advocates of teachers working together in order to change both the instructional climate and the culture of the school, but Joan would be the one working directly with the teacher leaders.

Sam believed strongly that teachers need to have a sense of accomplishment. Therefore, she urged teachers to develop a specific task or target, such as establishing a peer tutoring project, and a timeline so that they (and their colleagues) would be able to realize what they had set out to achieve. Sam also wanted exercising leadership to be fun for teachers. As she worked to get teachers district and state recognition for what they had accomplished, she found that teacher leadership work could be personally reinvigorating for teachers as well as provide "amazing opportunities for kids."

What were the challenges that Sam faced as she encouraged teacher leadership? She was frustrated when teachers demanded more resources than she could deliver. She understood the passion of the teacher leaders, but wished that they could understand that "change is a process, not an event." Although the teacher leaders were learning that they needed to switch from a very narrow to a broader, schoolwide perspective, their passion and impatience about their own initiatives translated into demands for more resources. Finally she told one teacher leader, "You have got to understand how much I am working for you, and you need to back off."

Sam also realized that some of the best teacher leaders face a conundrum when they consider how leadership activity affects their teaching. As a principal, she understood that they wanted their primary focus to be on their teaching, even while she was encouraging them to also be leaders in the school. As she noted:

> It's a dance between supporting and pushing them a little . . . Not everyone will like how you lead. It's important to help people navigate through [criticism and sniping from their peers] . . . Different people are going to lead in different ways and need to be supported in different ways. Some teachers need to be told to "go for it." Some teachers need to be stopped because they are going too fast.

Sam admitted that it can be challenging to entrust changes to a teacher. Since most principals are people who are comfortable with assuming control, it "can be scary to give up that control. But when I look at the ownership that develops, I know that it is worth the effort." The longer that Sam served as a high school principal, the more she became convinced that "shared leadership requires the ability to navigate and deal with the unexpected together."

When asked about incentives that could be offered for teacher leadership, Sam said, "People talk about monetary incentives, but for me, it's whether the teacher's time is well spent." Sam expressed that, besides providing resources for teachers' initiatives, it is important to have "someone to support them as they negotiate both [teaching and leadership] roles." In the end, she felt that the best incentive for teacher leaders was "seeing other people having an idea and being successful."

« « » »

The principals and teacher leaders in these two settings—a small urban school and a large suburban one—were working in different cultures and contexts. The urgency of the work and the small size of the mission-driven urban school made it necessary to develop focused, common learning objectives and instructional approaches as the principal and faculty worked to narrow the achievement gap. This was not so much the case in the large suburban high school, where the principals were able to build in some flexibility in a decentralized model while insisting that teachers meet to collaborate on learning.

Yet there are some similar aspects in how Monique and Sam approached the issue of teacher leadership in these two different schools. Both administrative leaders acknowledged they could not solve the instructional and other challenges in their schools by themselves. These principals wanted to hear from strong-willed teachers who would periodically disagree with and challenge them. Neither of them believed that she had all the answers, and they were both inclusive in their administrative style. As a result, teachers generously responded with their ideas, energy, and caring as they worked together to improve learning for all students.

While Monique was able to work directly with the faculty in her small school to encourage and develop teacher leaders, the size of Sam's suburban school prevented such direct interactions on a regular basis. She appointed Joan as vice principal, whose responsibilities included developing teacher leaders who would help establish a professional learning community. Joan provided the momentum and oversight to the teacher leaders, whose responsibilities were to reflect with colleagues about how to improve curriculum, assessments, and best practices in order to narrow "the identified economic and racially based" academic achievement gap. In each of these schools, the principal—a key person with authority—worked to encourage teacher leadership.

Both of these women principals had learned about organizational development, partly by participating in administrative preparation programs. They demonstrated transparency, which empowered their teachers. They also provided mentoring and professional development—which enabled teacher leaders to gain facilitation and other skills—and concrete resources such as time for teams to meet.

» ASHA
Building a Learning Community in a Charter School

We have just noted the impact that school size can have on principal/teacher relationships, but it's also important to recognize that charter school leaders may face different challenges to working with their teachers. And as charter schools expand their numbers, it is important to consider how they are supporting or discouraging teacher leadership.

Asha, a principal in what is acknowledged as a successful Boston-area charter school, has thought long and hard about the kinds of challenges she and other leaders face if they want to attract and retain the most effective teachers. She believes that teachers, as the primary stakeholders and workers in a school, need to feel that:

+ They are set up to do a great job;

- They have support and some autonomy to innovate;
- Their voices are heard and their needs are met;
- They have direct data about how their students are doing so that they can improve their instruction;
- They are invested in creating systems for continuously improving the organization.

Just as dedicated teachers often focus on becoming the kind of teacher that they would have wanted as a student, Asha's goal as an administrator is to become the kind of leader she would like to have had when she began teaching. In her quest to recruit and keep the best teachers in her charter school, she has created formal and informal structures to solicit teacher input. She welcomes dialogue and questions about what the school should be doing. A person with strong opinions, she has worked hard to convey that she would like to hear opposing ideas, although she would prefer to air disagreements *before* the school implements an idea.

> As a leader you often have to move, but that movement isn't going to be as good unless you have someone opposing [you] and pointing out the holes. It's really helpful to have a broader team with teacher leaders. If I have confidence that someone is going to oppose my idea, I can just throw myself into that move. I don't have to second-guess myself.

She has learned to recognize which decisions are priorities that should be discussed with all teachers—although she worries about achieving balance between empowerment and overempowerment, because "I can't do my job if I have to get weigh-in from thirty-six people on every single decision I make." Yet she also knows that "if [you] make a strong move as a leader, because they support you and they're invested and believe you have the same goals, they may hold back from opposing in that moment. And then the opposition happens in small conversations afterwards."

Asha gives an example of a decision made at the end of one year when she recommended that student detention be made "more painful," which the staff appeared to support.

And it really backfired in our face . . . it created this "us-versus-them" men-tality with some of the kids who were chronic offenders. Then I heard in small conversations people say, you know, the reason they were in deten-tion is because they just need more help . . . And it reminded me that if I had presented this in a setting where I'd heard people's input before mak-ing a plan, that would have come out.

Asha believes an effective leader needs to anticipate and understand his or her impact on others. Although she processes information very quickly, she recognizes now that she and those who coach in her school need to understand that some teachers think about dilemmas and ques-tions more slowly. Therefore, she needed to build in time to let ideas per-colate before she moves on to a decision.

Asha is not a laissez-faire administrator. Her charter school is very structured, with a consistent approach about instruction, curriculum, and student expectations. She believes that structures are necessary to create a level of professional autonomy. She gives every teacher weekly feedback on their lesson plans and has led the school to develop com-mon ways to address institutional and instructional challenges.

We've decided as a team that this is the way we're going to do it . . . If teachers feel that this is no longer the most efficient system, we revise it and make it a better one. So, we're not attached to the systems themselves. The goal of the systems is to create structures that allow teachers to channel all of their energy and creativity into actually pro-ducing results.

Unlike many charter school leaders and policy makers, however, she recognizes that it takes more than two years to become a good teacher. Therefore, Asha is committed to finding ways for teachers to want to be at a charter school for ten or twenty years. Her school created a Sus-tainability and Balance Working Group that focuses on how to sup-port teachers in various developmental stages of their families and careers, including supporting those who want to become teacher lead-ers. She notes:

Ambitious people need milestones in their career[s] and thus there must be various levels of empowerment for teachers who demonstrate leadership. And there must be support inside and/or outside for these teacher leaders as they encounter resistance, take on tasks that may grow to be unmanageable, or reflect on whether they want to be doing these in-between teacher leader roles.

Asha appreciates the freedom that she has to not renew teachers since all of the teachers have a one-year contract. Although she might also like to be able to offer three- to five-year contracts—because each time a good teacher leaves "it's a huge loss for me"—she realizes that, if she tried to create financial incentives so that teachers would stay in the charter school for fifteen years, "I could never afford that." Asha and other innovative charter school leaders who have a vision about creating a learning community that works for the adults as well as the students have much to think about as these schools evolve and become more established.

REFLECTIONS

This book affirms the importance of teachers having their voices heard and their needs met, but acknowledges that there are real challenges involved for both the principal and teacher leaders. For example, how does a principal create a culture where teachers and administrators can trust each other? What is the responsibility of teachers to contribute to such trust? How can a principal create an organizational culture where teachers offer their opinions and contributions *before* she or he has to make a decision, rather than hearing the complaints in parking lot conversations afterwards? Which decisions should be subject to deliberation—because "I can't do my job if I have to get weigh-in from thirty-six people on every single decision I make"?

It is not by chance that a couple of the stories in this chapter focus on principals leading small urban alternative or charter schools. The growth of these small urban schools offers opportunities for young teachers who want to become school leaders. However, just as teachers need to think about whether a school is a good fit, a principal in a small urban school who is committed to supporting teacher leadership needs to consider how to support teachers in a school so focused on student goals. Will she or he take on the challenge of being the thoughtful leader who will devote time to consulting with her teachers around priorities and decision making?

As the stories in this chapter indicate, principals who want to be effective at encouraging teacher leadership must have and be able to articulate a philosophy or vision that such leadership is important. In contrast to administrators or policy makers who believe in a top-down business model and think that they have figured out all that is needed to lead a school, these principals believe that teachers must have support and some autonomy to innovate; teachers' voices must be heard. They want to work with strong teachers who understand that teaching is complicated and challenging, and that it is important for teachers to be able to reflect and learn with colleagues who are good at their craft.

We have read about principals and teacher leaders facing challenges and opportunities in different contexts. Monique, the principal who helped create the Mandela School for Social Democracy in New York City, had previously participated as a teacher and administrator in a school that had encouraged teacher leadership. Because she knew that she wanted to create a school built on teacher involvement, she was looking for teachers who would share her vision. Thus, when Michael was selected to join one of the early groups of teachers, he knew that he was joining a team where *all* teachers were expected to be mentors and contributors inside and outside the classroom.

Sam's story is quite different. When she was appointed principal of Northern High School, a large, well-established, and respected suburban high school, she realized that she could not have a direct impact on developing teacher leadership. When Sam appointed Joan, an assistant who brought different skills, temperament, and priorities that complemented her own strengths and weaknesses, she was acknowledging that she could not do it all herself. The team of two principals, in consultation with department heads, was able to divide up the tasks, with Joan assuming responsibility for the support of teacher leadership. Thus, this is a story about distributing leadership, building capacity, and finding the right-size teams who could work together for change in this large school. Yet this principal, who conceived of her task as providing resources for teacher initiatives, still had to tell some teachers to slow down and "back off."

As we reflect on the stories in this chapter, it is possible to notice that even principals who led in very different schools shared some common approaches to their interactions with teacher leaders. In both the small mission-driven urban and larger suburban school, at least one administrator needed to provide vision and expectations for teacher leadership, as well as continue the institutional support that was essential to making the teacher leadership initiative part of the school's culture, or "the way we do things around here." It appears that teacher leadership becomes a high priority in a school only if it is a significant priority for at least one person who has power and access to resources.

School leaders who want to establish a professional learning community must provide time and space for the principal and teachers to learn from and support each other, and for teachers to have opportunities to learn from their colleagues. This will happen only if principals:

+ Can articulate and implement a vision of inclusive teacher leadership;
+ Establish the conditions under which teachers can gradually assume responsibility and power, take some risks, and be mentored to learn from their mistakes;
+ Are willing either to provide time, accessibility, and resources to support such leadership, or to assign someone else with power and resources to facilitate it.

Furthermore, principals need to help teacher leaders learn skills and dispositions that enable them to function effectively in an instructional institution that is part of a larger political context. This involves helping teacher leaders understand how the school functions as an organization, and what their options are when they make mistakes or encounter resistance. (This may be an area where higher education programs could provide some useful training.)

Principals also need to anticipate that they may be asked to resolve conflicts and dilemmas. For example, the selection of teacher leaders may raise difficulties for the principal. Teachers sometimes ask (or complain in the teachers' room): "Why did the principal select *her* for this task? She hasn't been here long enough to understand how we operate." "Is she the principal's favorite? Do I have to do what she wants?" This is one of the reasons why it is so important for principals to be transparent about their decision-making processes. Principals also need to help teacher leaders think about how they will be perceived (and want to be seen) as individuals and colleagues. This visibility means they will no longer have the comfort of simply being part of the larger group of teachers.

The actual form of teacher involvement and leadership will undoubtedly vary according to the school context: small or large, urban, rural, or suburban. Whatever the context, however, there need to be both formal and informal ways to encourage contributions and dialogue inside and outside a school. As Asha has noted, there must be systems in place that allow teachers to do excellent work and to have their voices heard and their needs met. Teacher leaders must have some autonomy and support to innovate within a system of shared responsibility and accountability.

Since teachers are going to be looking to principals for clues about their openness to suggestions, school leaders need to be transparent about the process of and reasons behind their decision making. As Monique realized, a principal needs to consider how to institutionalize support so that the school's teacher leadership is not dependent solely on one administrator, who may move on to another role or school.

Principals should also consider how to acknowledge the additional work that teacher leaders do. Monique, Sam, and Asha have given recognition to teachers and worked to provide resources that would support their initiatives. It would also be helpful to acknowledge teacher leaders' pleas for time, and if possible, relieve these educators of some teaching responsibilities as a way of supporting their work as both teachers and leaders in the school.

If we want teacher leaders to become invested in creating systems for continuously improving the organization, principals and directors of schools need to be open to listening to those who may disagree with them, without allowing opposing voices to stop initiatives. A principal or director who encourages innovative and questioning educators will go far in creating a learning community that cherishes students, teachers, and the communities they are serving.

In addition, principals and teacher leaders can learn from the examples of practitioners who are experimenting with different models to reform schools. Which models are succeeding? How are they resolving different challenges? In the next chapter, we will read about teachers leading in three very different contexts: acting as cobuilding leaders of an alternative middle school in Ohio; being part of turnaround teams in urban schools; and leading district courses that build colleagues' skills and competencies in Boston.

We are learning from our work that the largest share of the challenge of teacher leadership roles comes not from being able to carry out work tasks skillfully, but from workplace variables that make it challenging to carry them out at all.

—Jill Harrison Berg and Phomdaen Souvanna[1]

5 FORMALIZING TEACHER LEADERSHIP

Three Emerging Models

THIS CHAPTER EXAMINES three secondary-level formal models of teacher leadership, where roles are conceived and structured differently from the informal and semiformal instructional roles described in previous chapters. Two of these models were created by teachers; each has the goal of helping teacher voices to be heard. The teacher leaders participating in these new models want power to shape the institutional contexts in which they are working *and* to have more control over their profession.

In the first part of this chapter, you will read about two teacher leaders who become the administrative leaders of an alternative suburban middle school in Ohio. This kind of school-based leadership position often develops gradually and organically, building on teachers' commitment to improve instructional or institutional functioning within their own schools. The experience of teachers implementing a shared administrative model feels new to the educators who develop it in each school (although there are other teacher-run schools in Boston, Milwaukee, and Los Angeles). It makes sense that the educators in each teacher-run school would want to shape such a model to fit their schools' particular culture and context.

In contrast to this home-grown model, some outside reformers are seeking to develop urban teacher leaders as part of turnaround schools' efforts. We will examine the stories of teachers selected to be part of a cohort working with a principal in a "turnaround" school, and of collaborative course facilitators developed by the Boston Teacher Leadership Resource Center (BTLRC).

Teachers in more formal leadership roles developed by district or outside reformers usually receive more training and external support, but their goals may be constrained. Many are evaluated based on their ability to achieve certain specific goals, such as raising student achievement on state assessments. This model can raise questions about whether the leadership tasks are defined too narrowly, leaving teachers little space and authority to respond to unanticipated issues or to strengthen the school culture. Moreover, unless the focus on improving instruction is coupled with organizational changes, such initiatives may not have a lasting impact.

Teacher leaders must be knowledgeable about how to mobilize colleagues who may not share their enthusiasm for yet another change initiative. Teacher leadership roles often raise questions about relationships among colleagues once a teacher is elevated to have more power, including in some cases being asked to contribute to another teacher's evaluation. Does this change in status erode trust among former colleagues? After all, if teachers are not willing to be led or to work together to change teaching and learning, leadership positions will not be perceived as effective.

» WALNUT MIDDLE SCHOOL

A Teacher-Led Alternative School

Liz and Patrick are co–teacher leaders at the Walnut Middle School, a small alternative middle school in Ohio with 160 seventh and eighth graders and sixteen faculty members. Liz and Patrick are both in their fifties. Liz, a former elementary school teacher and librarian, is the mother of two college-aged students; she is an outstanding and wise educator. Patrick, a physical education and special education teacher, has the build of an athlete and the no-nonsense demeanor of a dean, which is the role he filled previously in a middle school. When district administrators asked for proposals for what to do with extra building capacity due to declining enrollment, Liz was part of a group of ten teachers whose proposal to create a small alternative school with mastery-based and individualized learning for seventh and eighth graders was selected.

The story of the Walnut Middle School is similar to those of many small schools in urban and suburban districts that have been created by teachers with a vision. Liz notes that the small group of self-selected founding teachers had an entrepreneurial spirit; they loved challenge and change. In order to create a school where all students would have more time and support to master skills and knowledge, they proposed creating an integrated and experiential curriculum and a schedule that would extend the school day for an additional two hours. Teachers and students would volunteer to be part of this alternative school. Liz says: "We understood that we were not getting paid more . . . We knew that we just needed more time with kids." Although the union opposed their working longer hours without an additional stipend, the teachers signed forms confirming their willingness to do this.

The teachers who submitted the proposal were experienced and respected educators. Patrick noted: "I think one thing that really works for us is our experience and how long we've been around . . . All our names were strong in the district for a long time. So, we kind of knew each other by reputation, before we'd even worked together." While they were willing to take a risk by creating a new school, the experience they had gained through teaching in the district for many years brought credibility to their plans for the new school.

Reflecting on the school's beginning years, Liz and Patrick report that they faced two different kinds of challenges. The first involved the alternative school's relationship to the more traditional middle school, with which they shared a space. There were teachers and community members who blamed the Walnut School for the eventual decision to close the more traditional middle school—the growing enrollment at the alternative school offering a stark contrast to the declining enrollment at the traditional middle school. Rich, who was serving as the principal of both the larger middle school and Walnut Middle School, helped manage these conflicts during the transition. Once it became clear that the larger school was going to be closed down, Rich became a half-time principal to Walnut Middle School and worked for the district in his remaining time. He encouraged the alternative school's teachers to focus on the school's vision and commitment to faculty *and* student problem solving.

The second problem was related to the strengths and weaknesses of the school's teaching team. It is not surprising that teachers attracted to the idea of creating a new middle school were outspoken individuals with strong ideas about curriculum. They came together with an instructional vision, but not a detailed concrete plan for how their institution would function. As a result, they needed to find ways to work together and resolve disagreements. During their Friday afternoon faculty meetings, the discussions would sometimes go on and on, until Patrick became so frustrated that he began to draw up agendas for subsequent meetings. The faculty needed to learn how to balance listening to all voices in a democratic school with making decisions and being efficient with their time at the end of a very full week.

As they were working out these two challenges, the staff learned that they were going to lose their principal. When the district began to encounter financial problems, the superintendent decided to move Rich to the central office, although he would continue to be the part-time principal of the school. A question then arose about who would provide on-site leadership. After Rich talked with Liz and Patrick about the possibility of their becoming co–teacher leaders in the school, he consulted with the rest of the faculty about the appointments. Rich proposed that the co–teacher leaders would divide the administrative responsibilities, except for teacher evaluations, which he would continue to do. He asked the faculty to think about it for a week; they reconvened and approved the arrangement in a subsequent faculty meeting.

This was a new way of conceiving of teacher leader roles within the district. There were other teacher leader positions, but they were full-time assignments in the district office. (These were often seen as positions en route to administrative openings.) Patrick had been the dean in the more traditional school, and Liz did not have administrative certification; nor did she want to leave the classroom. Moreover, the proposal was that Liz and Patrick would continue as full-time teachers with five classes, with teacher leader responsibilities added on. They were each paid a small yearly stipend of $5,000 to assume their respective additional instructional and administrative responsibilities.

Charles Kerchner, who has studied teacher-run schools in Milwaukee, writes that "much of the relationship between the teacher-run schools and the district has existed as informal permission, where formal authority rests with the district, but operating discretion rests with the school."[2] A similar division of tasks and authority was adopted in this Ohio school, where the administrative/teacher leader structure has worked well. Patrick is responsible for discipline and building operations, and parents come to him with their problems. Faculty and staff look to Liz for instructional leadership. Her responsibilities include curricular issues, testing, professional development, library media, and instructional technology. Their full-time teaching assignments make it challenging for the two school leaders to serve as liaisons between the school and district office. Therefore, Rich assumes this responsibility, as well as the teacher evaluations. (Their full-time teaching responsibilities mean that the two teacher leaders usually miss district training and opportunities to participate directly in district discussions about issues such as the district schedule for testing that could have an impact on their school.)

One of the reasons that this co–teacher leadership model is effective is that everyone at this school chooses to be there: the faculty, the students, and the teacher leaders. Patrick says about the school's very strong faculty:

Everybody pitches in. To be a strong teacher leader, it's a lot like a coach. Great players make great coaches. Well, great teachers make great teacher leaders. We just have our hand on the rudder.

In the Walnut Middle School, major decisions are made either by the faculty or with faculty input. The co—teacher leaders have learned when it is helpful to let the dialogue continue and when one of them needs to declare that a decision has been made.

Patrick and Liz had the experience and confidence to be effective co—teacher leaders. After several years of learning from Rich when he was principal, they knew how to divide up the tasks in a way that played to their strengths. They worked incredibly hard, and their styles complemented each other. They were both also at a place in their careers that made them ready for this challenge. Both of these faculty members had credibility as very strong educators. They also developed new skills as they assumed leadership responsibilities.

Liz says that the arrangement worked well because "you've got two people who don't need power." She could devote the time and energy to being successful in this position because she no longer had young children. Patrick believes that this role worked for him because he was at a point in his career when

> I come in every day; I work for 160 kids. I do what I honestly feel in my heart is right, and I really don't care what anybody else says. Nobody is going to come back at me, because what are you going to do? Fire me and take my $5,000? You're going to stick me in a gym for the rest of my career, where I just have to shoot baskets?

Patrick's role was easier for parents and teachers to understand, because he assumed the tasks that parents expect a principal would do: discipline, building operations, special education coordination. It is noteworthy that Liz's instructional leadership role was at times less clear to the community and some of her colleagues. Perhaps this was because teachers were much more eager to assume responsibility for curriculum and instruction, and glad to delegate discipline and building operations to Patrick. There was at least one teacher who questioned why Liz should get paid a $5,000 stipend when they were all doing instructional and curriculum work. When this question was raised, Liz reflected that she was "really grateful that I am fifty years old, and that I have a lot more confidence than I used to." Partly because of this, though, she began to take on more responsibilities, such as student recruitment and scheduling, by herself.

This school worked because of the trust that developed among the strong core of faculty members, the two co-leaders' readiness to assume leadership responsibilities, the mentoring of the former principal, and the willingness of the two faculty leaders to take on additional work and responsibilities for nominal pay. Students were achieving success as measured by standardized tests; the seventh and eighth graders were also doing the kind of creative problem solving and experiential learning that made them want to come to school.

Ronald Heifetz and Marty Linsky describe how important it is for leaders to climb on the balcony and see what the dance floor looks like.[3] This was very difficult for the two co-leaders, with their full-time teaching responsibilities combined with the daily leadership tasks. Despite these day-to-day challenges, however, they were beginning to move away from being absorbed by institutional functioning to considering a peer evaluation program that would enable the faculty to examine their instructional practice with each other.

The Walnut Middle School provides an example of teacher leadership that grew organically. The adults in this school created a culture based on their mission to develop a strong learning community for young people and the adults who are educating them. This school, which met the district's as well as its own needs, arose from teachers who were acknowledged instructional experts. A group of teachers wanted to create an exciting alternative school that seventh and eighth graders would want to attend, and that their parents would want to select. The co—teacher leader model also saved the district money, because a principal did not have to be hired for this small school.

Even though they have been very deliberate in thinking about how co-leaders fit into the school culture they have created, Liz and Patrick do not picture themselves as creating a model of teacher leadership for others to emulate. It is not clear if or how the school's culture will change once either of the two original teacher leaders retires. Although others considering using teacher leaders to run a school could learn from their experiences, part of the strength of this model is that it was developed organically within a very specific context. (There are other teacher-run schools that have been developed as part of the EdVisions Cooperative and the Boston and Los Angeles Pilot Schools.) Those who would develop a similar school and leadership team will need to create and frame such a school so that it fits their own context and community.

» TURNAROUND TEACHER TEAMS
Empowering a Cohort of Teachers

In contrast to that home-grown school, we will now examine some urban school models that have been developed because federal and state governments are desperate to find ways to reform the lowest performing urban schools and improve student achievement. Reformers are developing different "turnaround" models based on an understanding of how challenging it can be to teach in K–12 classrooms, especially some in high-need schools. In this section, we will examine a model constructed on social capital, where a principal and a Turnaround Teacher Team (T3)—a chosen cohort of teacher leaders—join together to improve a struggling urban school. This model has been piloted in Boston, Massachusetts, and then expanded to Fall River, Massachusetts, and Memphis, Tennessee. It is not surprising that it was a group of Boston teachers participating in the Teaching Policy Fellowship of the organization Teach Plus who wrote the proposal, *Ready for the Next Challenge*.[4] (Teach Plus is an advocacy organization devoted to encouraging the voices of second-stage teachers "to improve outcomes for urban children by ensuring that a greater proportion of students have access to effective, experienced teachers ... We work with both results-oriented teachers and education policy leaders in transforming the profession to reward excellence and results."[5]) This proposal envisioned the Teacher Turnaround Team (T3) cohort model as a way to address both student academic underachievement *and* the loss of effective teachers in schools with a history of persistently low student achievement. Their idea was that it takes a team of very strong, experienced teachers, in addition to an excellent principal, to turn a school around. Meghan O'Keefe, national director of T3, notes:

> The teachers who wrote the proposal all got into teaching to work with the highest-need kids, but they wanted to make sure certain conditions [were] in place before they left where they were and went to one of the lower performing schools. The conditions outlined in the proposal were: they wanted to go as part of a team. They wanted to know they were going to have a group of colleagues who were moving in the same direction, and they would have critical mass. They wanted to have formal leadership roles. They didn't want to leave the classroom, but they wanted to be able to take on formal leadership roles. They wanted to work for a strong principal who believed in teacher leadership and distributing some authority to teachers. They wanted to make sure that the other services kids would need would be in place, and they put additional compensation on the list, not that they thought that was the most important thing, but as a signal that this work was valued.

Massachusetts defines level 3 and 4 schools as those that have performed poorly on state assessments in mathematics and English language arts and have not shown substantial improvement. The Boston Public Schools decided to use School Improvement Grant and Race to the Top funds to subcontract with Teach Plus to develop a cohort of teacher leaders who would work alongside a principal to change the culture and teaching in some of Boston's level 3 and 4 schools. In 2011, the Boston Public School District began implementing the T3 turnaround model in three Boston Public Schools, and extended it to another three schools the following year.

The T3 model, which is one of several turnaround models that Boston is using, gives a team of teachers power and responsibility to help change the culture of a school and improve student achievement. The first step is to recruit and select effective and experienced urban teachers who want to work collaboratively with others. The selection process involves T3 staff, district staff, and principals, who participate in the interview days. (At first, T3 was able to use an innovative staffing model because state-passed legislation allowed level 4 schools to bypass some union requirements for staffing and the length of the school day. In level 4 schools, they were able to restaff the schools with approximately one third of the teachers already in the partner school, one third from other Boston schools, and one third from teachers outside the district. They do not have this freedom with level 3 schools, and have to use naturally occurring vacancies to create their T3 cohorts.)

O'Keefe says that they select T3 teacher leaders based on criteria that "include a minimum of three years' full-time teaching experience, a track record of effectiveness with urban or high-poverty students, and some history of leadership roles." She notes that they consciously chose some teachers who were in the school to join the T3 team because they did not want to "set up an us-versus-them" dynamic. The motivation of teachers joining the first cohort varied. The cohort included some fairly young teachers and others with as much as twenty-five years of teaching experience, who, according to O'Keefe,

> . . . were looking for the next challenge, but weren't going to go to one of the worse performing schools in the city unless it was part of a program, so that they'd know that they would have the support to be successful there, and have colleagues who wanted to do the work as well.

The average level of experience of T3 teacher leaders is nine years.

Once selected, each T3 member is assigned to a specific leadership role, such as leading a grade-level or subject team. As O'Keefe points out, the T3 cohort is trained in "strategies that have been used by other highly effective teacher teams." There is also a part-time coach for each school who gives day-to-day support to the T3 teacher leaders to help them work effectively with other teachers during the school year. O'Keefe says:

> The goal is not to have 25 percent of the classrooms be staffed with effective teachers, but to make sure that those teacher leaders are working with the other teachers in such a way that they're *all* improving.

As in charter schools, the principal and T3 teacher leaders in these turnaround schools are unified around a shared mission. The designers of this model recognize that if instruction is going to improve, reflective and knowledgeable teachers must lead data-based conversations with their colleagues on how curriculum and instruction are or are not working with the children they are teaching and how they should change. It is not yet clear whether the model will focus on issues beyond the articulation of curriculum, instruction, and assessment, but what they are doing currently is a definite improvement over what had been happening previously in these hard-to-staff schools.

The expectation is that school structures will change because T3 teams "have additional time for collaboration, meetings with coaches and mentor teachers; data analysis tools and support; and the opportunity to attend summer institutes and complete additional course work."[6] Principals, however, may differ on how they choose to utilize and integrate the T3 teams within the school and their leadership team, and the funding that provides resources for the T3 teams currently is only for a three-year span.

It is difficult to gauge the effectiveness of the T3 model with only two years of data. Although the value-added results for students are positive, they are not uniformly so among the schools using this model. This is not surprising, as these schools have different cultures, students and faculty, and contexts. What is promising, however, is that this model is designed to improve some of the working conditions in struggling schools, which Johnson, Kraft, and Papay's research concludes has a positive impact on student achievement:

> Furthermore, although a wide range of working conditions matter to teachers, the specific elements of the work environment that matter the most to teachers are not narrowly conceived "working conditions" such as clean and well-maintained facilities or access to modern institutional technology. Instead, it is the social conditions—the school's culture, the principal's leadership, and relationships among colleagues—that predominate in predicting teachers' job satisfaction and career plans.[7]

Unlike a top-down hierarchical model, where the emphasis is primarily on the principal as the instructional leader who will turn around a school, the T3 model envisions change as coming through appointed teacher leaders as well as from a principal who is a strong instructional leader. The T3 initiative offers a path toward mastery in urban teaching and teacher leadership, and combined with turnaround schools' longer school day for all students and teachers, it enables more effective teaching and learning. The formal teacher leader role in turnaround schools has been negotiated with the Boston Teachers Union: each T3 teacher leader is paid an additional $6,000/year for the time equivalent of twenty-five additional days of school. (The funds come from School Improvement Grants, and there is not yet a decision about whether these stipends will be maintained once the grant ends.) This stipend recognizes that teacher leaders are doing more work and are part of the formal leadership team at the school.

However, some questions about the T3 model persist. This model does raise concerns about whether the T3 teams create a new, privileged subgroup of teachers. Do some teachers have more agency and voice than others? The T3 staff continue to stress to new T3 faculty team members that there are many other teacher leaders whom they must respect as colleagues in the schools where they are working. They also encourage teachers within the school to apply to join their team. Nonetheless, there is undoubtedly some resentment among teachers outside of the team about the T3 teachers' stipends and access to power. How does this affect collegiality and trust among the faculty? Do the T3 teachers get sufficient training and support during the year to address these challenges? Should there be some structural safeguards so that questioning and dissident teacher voices can be heard without fear of exclusion or of being transferred out of the school?

Although the explicit goal of the T3 teams is to improve instruction, the T3 organization has found that it cannot ignore institutional challenges raised when the teams begin to work in the schools. If the three-year timetable for additional resources for turnaround schools is extended, will there be opportunities for teachers who are not in the original T3 team to rotate in and out and become part of the leadership group? (It is promising that when one of the first T3 schools expanded, they added additional T3 teacher leaders from within the school.) If the timetable is not extended, how will positive changes be sustained once the additional funds and staffing end? Finally, will policy makers understand why implementation and results vary according to the context and culture of individual schools?

As they move to answer these questions, the Teach Plus leaders are being careful to expand to other schools and districts only as quickly as they feel they can support the model well. Reformers would do well to follow the T3 schools closely, as they are part of a districtwide model that is designed with the flexibility to allow the teams to be responsive to different school contexts. It will be especially interesting to see whether student accomplishments (measured by various kinds of assessments), as well as instructional reforms, will be sustained after the formal initiative ends.

» COLLABORATIVE COACHING AND LEARNING
Systemic Support for Teacher Leadership Development

A third model has emerged in the Boston Public Schools, which have a substantial history of tapping teacher leaders to strengthen teaching and learning. Under former superintendent Thomas Payzant's leadership, the district decided to use Annenberg Foundation funds to provide extensive support for teachers through Collaborative Coaching and Learning (CCL):

> Known as Collaborative Coaching and Learning, the approach provides in-school, in-classroom support from coaches skilled in content areas, along with time for teachers to collaborate with one another and the coaches to analyze student data, observe model lessons, try out model lessons, and reflect on their practices together.[8]

In the process of implementing this model, however, the district and others soon realized that many teachers on the CCL teams did not know how to lead. While some were very competent, others were being asked to do tasks for which they had no training. Therefore, in 2009, the Boston Plan for Excellence (now the BPE), the Boston Public Schools, and the Boston Teacher Residency (BTR) applied for federal Teacher Quality Partnership funds to create a resource center for teacher leaders that would be led by Boston teachers respected for their experience and expertise. The premise of the resource center was that "a systemic approach is needed so that teacher leadership capacity is no longer built individually, but collectively; so that teacher leadership is an organizational asset capable of fueling reform."[9] It is useful to review how this initiative to build urban teacher leader expertise has fared.

Jill Harrison Berg, the director of the Boston Teacher Leadership Resource Center (BTLRC), says that the center began with two main goals: (1) to establish a training component that would enable teacher leaders to develop the leadership skills required in their roles; and (2) to design tools and resources that can help leaders create conditions within schools that will support teacher leadership. Berg pulled together two different groups of Boston educators to plan and implement these two different, but complementary initiatives.

After examining national and state standards for teacher leaders, the planning group for the teacher training component created a series of courses to help teacher leaders develop "a range of specialized skills, beyond those required for effective classroom teaching." Berg and Souvanna write:

> In order to identify the knowledge, skills and competencies that would become the content of the program, they pursued a backward-planning approach: They looked at the specific tasks required by four locally significant teacher leadership roles and used their review of research and existing programs to create a comprehensive list of what teachers would have to know and be able to do to succeed in these roles.[10]

Berg and the resource center staff worked with teachers to create four collaborative courses as the central offerings of the Boston Teacher Leadership Certificate Program. Teachers were treated as respected professionals who would design and teach courses for their colleagues.

Those teachers who attended the courses were self-selected and held a variety of teacher leader roles in the district. Unlike traditional graduate courses, the collaborative courses were facilitated study groups that were "competency-based . . . dynamic and responsive" to the participants' strengths and learning goals. Since they focused on helping teachers to fulfill particular responsibilities, the courses were immediately relevant to participants. Teachers were able to earn the certificate after they had demonstrated their competency through performance assessments that showed their capability in one of the four areas: use of data, supporting instruction, shared leadership, and professional expertise.

After each session, participants reflected on what they had learned. Teacher leaders reported that they felt more effective both as teachers and as leaders, and also appreciated having a safe place where they could discuss the implementation challenges they faced as well as the successes they experienced and the support they received from each other. The courses helped participants gain new skills; they also enabled teachers to increase their pay, as they earned job-relevant credits and moved up the salary scale.

Even while they were thinking about the teacher leadership courses that the center would offer through its certificate program, Berg and others were quite aware of the uneven implementation and shelf life of past reform initiatives. They turned to principals and teachers who had been involved in these past initiatives to create an advisory committee that would focus on what kind of school conditions would make it possible for teacher leaders to be effective. This committee wrestled with a series of implementation questions, such as: What kind of job descriptions should be developed for teacher leader positions? What were reasonable task expectations when teachers were already feeling overwhelmed by increased instructional demands? How could they help principals understand what they should look for when appointing a strong teacher leader? How could strong principals and assertive teacher leaders work out power sharing? Should there be term limits for teachers to serve in these positions so that there would not be automatic assumptions about who would be appointed as a teacher leader year after year?

It is unfortunate that this part of the initiative faltered because of insufficient funding. The center posted on its Web site some information that interested principals might use to establish a good organizational culture, but they were not able to pursue the development of more tools or to provide support so that principals could learn to use them effectively. Without a systematic approach to resolving institutional challenges arising from teacher leadership, it is left up to individual principals who are interested (and who know about the Web site) to make use of the tools that the center has developed. Further, the work competes for school and district leaders' attention with other districtwide priorities, such as implementing a new teacher evaluation process and aligning with the Common Core. This is ironic, as teachers with strong leadership skills could be effective resources in implementing these other initiatives. Berg and Souvanna's research concludes that:

> We are learning from our work that the largest share of the challenge of teacher leadership roles comes not from being able to carry out work tasks skillfully, but from workplace variables that make it challenging to carry them out at all. If teachers do not have the resources they need, the authority to put what they are learning to use, or a school culture that can support the learning to take hold, their roles will have limited impact and teachers will grow frustrated. Under these conditions, teacher leadership can lead to the attrition of teachers instead of their retention.[11]

This story is not a new one for Boston or other school districts. In the last decade, when urban school districts have faced very difficult budgetary cutbacks, instructional coaches that were the center of the Collaborative Coaching and Learning (CCL) initiative were eliminated, even as instructional demands on teachers to improve student achievement mounted. Such school-based, embedded, and effective professional development no longer supports struggling teachers across the Boston Public Schools, because the district had to make some very tough decisions about the allocation of limited resources in order to keep classroom teachers on staff.

Meanwhile, the BTLRC model was limited in its scope and effectiveness, and was not able to address ways to change the organizational and political conditions in the schools where teacher leaders are asked to function. In schools where conditions support teacher leadership, a real partnership is developing between the principal and teacher leaders; without this partnership, teacher leaders may struggle, become frustrated, and often abandon their efforts to improve their schools.

While the designers of this initiative knew when they began that they needed to address both the school conditions *and* the training that would strengthen teacher leader skills, issues with funding and a shift in district priorities have made it challenging to do so. This story indicates that reformers must address issues of sustainability and institutionalization. Although grant funds are appropriately used to pilot new programs, reliance on such funds becomes problematic when financial challenges and other pressing priorities compete for support. The initiative is then perceived as something good, but not essential for strengthening teaching and learning.

REFLECTIONS

There is a continuum of leadership activities available in different schools and contexts. Figure 5.1 illustrates some of these roles—moving from the informal to the more formal roles. It also includes several relatively new roles, such as member of a teacher turnaround team (T3) and facilitator of collaborative courses designed by teachers for teacher leaders.

This continuum may work in a number of ways. A teacher may have the opportunity to select which position makes the most sense for her or him, or a school may change its organization or culture and ask teachers to learn new skills and assume new roles. The informal roles depicted in the left and center columns of the chart have not been negotiated in a union contract, and teachers usually do not receive additional pay for this work. This informality can work well for those who want to move back and forth between their primary role as a teacher and an ad hoc role that contributes to instructional or institutional arenas. A teacher may want to devote all of her professional energy and focus to the classroom, or she could decide to move temporarily into a more visible teacher leader role. The informal structure offers a flexibility that affirms the centrality and importance of the teacher's work and contributions in the classroom. In

FIGURE 5.1

Continuum of teacher leader roles found in secondary schools

Informal ➡ **Formal**

Instructional leaders

Respected classroom teacher	Teacher researcher	Literacy or math coach
Teacher who makes suggestions about professional development and/or school culture	Participant in Rounds or Critical Friends Group	Board-certified teacher
	Instructional team member	BTLRC collaborative course facilitator
Teacher willing to experiment with new instruction/technology	Mentor to beginning teacher	Member of T3 cohort

Institutional leaders

Teacher who makes suggestions about teachers, students, the community, and/or school culture	Community member working to improve school	Data team leader
	Occasional workshop presenter	T3 group leader
	Teacher who is consulted re decisions	Union representative
	Teacher researcher	Co–teacher leader of school
	Active union member	Peer Assistance and Review (PAR) team member

contrast, the roles in the third column are formal roles for which teachers apply and can receive a title and additional pay.

There are advantages and disadvantages to the informal or semiformal secondary school teacher leader roles. While they provide flexibility and an opportunity to contribute and to be heard within a school, informal leadership roles do require teachers to take on responsibilities above and beyond their primary work in the classroom. Asking teachers to volunteer their efforts again and again can become problematic. Teachers are quite aware that their salaries are not very generous compared to those in other professions that require a graduate degree. The level of pay is not only important in and of itself, it is also symbolic of whether the career of teaching is respected in this country. Given the prevailing widespread criticism and lack of appreciation of teachers, they may be reluctant to volunteer for still more work. In addition, the lack of training and the isolation in which many teacher leaders find themselves can make them feel as though they must address problems by themselves. If their problem-solving strategies do not work, they may judge themselves to be inadequate.

(Please note that this chapter does not begin to examine all of the new urban teacher leadership roles being developed or those that are modified versions of older forms of teacher leadership. For example, Peer Assistance and Review (PAR) programs represent an important step by the American Federation of Teachers (AFT) to move toward accountability for teacher performance. A panel composed of AFT teachers and administrators identifies struggling teachers, works with an identified teacher to develop a plan and support, and provides resources to help the teacher. If he or she does not improve, the panel recommends that the teacher be dismissed, even if the teacher is tenured. PAR and the three models of teacher leadership discussed in this chapter offer differentiated roles that develop the profession of teaching.)

We have read about two different approaches for developing teacher leadership—the home-grown model versus a systematic approach to reform schools. These models have different strengths and weaknesses. It might appear that the first model, which enabled two teachers to take on instructional or institutional administrative leadership, relates only to that specific school. Because the two school leaders were respected veteran teachers, they were able to work with their peers to develop and implement schoolwide programs based on the strengths and needs of their students and community. Such school-based roles offer space for teachers to develop a vision and implement change with others. It is tempting to dismiss this as an idiosyncratic approach that could not be brought to scale, but some teacher-run pilot schools in Los Angeles are being modeled after Boston teacher-run schools such as the Fenway High School and the K–8 Boston Teachers Union School.

The two Boston-based models, the T3 teams and the Boston Teacher Leadership Resource Center, which have been carefully designed to strengthen teaching and learning, are also dependent on school leadership and social capital. Those who are developing these models have more ambitious aims than improving instruction within one school. These models are being created and assessed as part of a larger outcome-based initiative to bring school and district reforms to scale. They also may be seen as part of a general initiative to change teaching into a differentiated profession where some educators will be selected and compensated for responsibilities other than classroom teaching.

As urban schools work to narrow the achievement gap among racial, ethnic, and socioeconomic groups, some reformers are interested in creating more formal teacher roles similar to the ones described in this chapter. These roles are being explored based on the belief that groups of teachers need to: (1) focus on evidence of student achievement; (2) posit and evaluate instructional changes to improve student achievement on state assessments; and (3) hold themselves accountable for what does and doesn't work.

However, too often national policy makers are acting on the hypothesis that urban schools can succeed despite the impacts of poverty on students and families—they just need to find the right principals, remove the "deadwood" teachers, and reward the good ones. Johnson, Kraft, and Papay's research questions the effectiveness of this approach:

> [M]any so-called turnaround schools downplay the importance of the social context in which teachers work and place heightened attention on individual teachers' effectiveness by offering financial incentives to teach at the school or insisting that successful teachers should be reassigned there. Our findings suggest that this narrow attention to the individual in isolation from the organization is misguided. Unless those schools become places where the principals and teachers can work together to build a school culture that supports good instruction, the much-sought-after gains in student learning will not be realized.[12]

Ignoring teachers' voices about the importance of working conditions, these policy makers have been searching for incentives to attract determined and talented individuals as principals and teachers who will be able to turn around struggling schools by themselves. This individualistic model is based on an assumption that competition and recognition through monetary incentives will draw and keep talented adults so that they are motivated to continue to work in such schools. Yet, while urban teachers and principals certainly appreciate being paid more handsomely, research does not conclude that merit pay and other individualistic approaches have a sustainable positive impact on student achievement.

In contrast to these nationally imposed and individualistic solutions, the models in this chapter have been developed either by or in consultation with teachers. They are models that acknowledge the importance of building on and affirming local initiatives and experiences.

When we compare the stories of the three developing teacher leader roles described in this chapter, there are some significant similarities. First, most of these teacher leaders are experienced educators. Their selection affirms the importance of the knowledge, skills, and perspectives they have gained during their time in the field. At a time when some proclaim that experience means little in assessing teacher effectiveness, these teacher leaders affirm the importance of experience, professional knowledge, and collaboration.

Second, it is not enough simply to be a good teacher; teacher leadership demands new skills and dispositions. Because teacher leaders work with adults rather than children, they need to understand adult development as well as the structure, human resources, politics, and culture of the school. Liz and Patrick had mentoring from their former principal. T3 teams have a school-based coach in addition to summer training, biweekly meetings with their cohort, and cross-school professional development sessions. The Boston Teacher Leadership Resource Center offered four collaborative coaching courses that developed skills and the opportunities for leaders to think together about their experiences in the field.

If teacher leaders are unprepared to face criticism from colleagues, they will probably take such resistance personally. And if principals and teachers do not understand that it takes time and real dialogue to enable colleagues to internalize changes in the school's culture and curriculum, they may confuse compliance with shared ownership of the change.

Third, none of these models depends on a heroic, single educator to reform a school. Neither the principal nor the teacher leaders are expected to do the work by themselves. Whether it is the two co-leaders working with the rest of the teachers at the Walnut Middle School, the T3 team, or the BTLRC's collaborative course facilitators designing and delivering graduate courses for their colleagues, these models affirm the need for a critical mass to support each other to create and deepen a collaborative culture. Given the complex and challenging work of changing classroom teaching and learning as well as school culture, it is clearly helpful to work with others.

(At the same time, it is important to note that there are some real differences in how these models are structured, and reformers should be paying closer attention to these structural differences. As Berg and Souvanna note, unless schools are set up to welcome and support teacher leadership, even those teacher leaders who are well trained will choose to exit the school and/or the profession if they are assigned to schools where they are ignored, undercut, or treated with hostility.)

Fourth, these stories raise questions about sustainability. What will the Walnut Middle School look like when the co-leaders retire? What is the plan for the turnaround schools and the teacher leaders once the three-year funding for T3 teams ends? How can reformers and school district leaders plan for institutionalization once the original funding ends for the BTLRC? Is teacher leadership a priority only during good financial times?

Those teacher leaders who are working with others to improve their schools are passionate about their work. Since so much of their time and energy is focused on their students, colleagues, and communities, many educators feel far removed from those who are making policy. Yet, as we will read in the next chapter, some teachers are beginning to share their opinions through networks and to insist that they become part of the larger educational dialogue. What is even more exciting is that some reformers and policy makers are beginning to listen.

The teacher leader understands the landscape of education policy and can identify key players at the local, state, and national levels. The teacher leader advocates for the teaching profession and for policies that benefit student learning.

—Domain VII, Teacher Leader Model Standards[1]

6 POLICY LEADERSHIP

Teachers' Voices Outside Schools

AS WE HAVE BEEN listening to teachers' voices about instruction and the kinds of structures and cultures that support their work, we have been examining their leadership within schools—the places where teachers work. In this chapter, we will examine how and why teacher leaders are raising their voices outside schools—whether in informal settings, professional networks, or advocacy organizations. Teachers, like many in today's technological world, are using the Internet to share resources and reflections about their work and students. They are also searching for safe arenas outside of school to discuss their work and their interactions with colleagues.

» TEACHER NETWORKS

Forums for Discussion and Opportunities for Leadership

The availability of horizontal and accessible networks has encouraged educators to write blogs that are read across the country. Educators are turning to networks to reflect on their work, to share resources, and to express frustration that, under the Race to the Top initiative, the locus of accountability has shifted from schools to teachers, who are being held individually responsible for how much their students have improved each year as measured by standardized tests. This policy shift reflects both the reality that schools will not be able to eliminate student achievement gaps by 2014 (as mandated by the No Child Left Behind Act in 2001) and the acknowledgment of the importance of teachers in their students' achievement. New education policies that focus on teachers have been accompanied by a continuous drumbeat of criticism that has blamed teachers and teacher unions for students' poor performance. As a result, some educators are seeking to be heard in venues that extend beyond the confines of their own buildings. We will consider why it has become increasingly important that those who want to improve education find ways to involve educators in the discussion of practice and policy, and how networks offer new possibilities for interactions among teachers.

Teachers spend so much time in schools that they often view the institution not just as a workplace, but also as a kind of family or adult community. In elementary schools, principals often refer to those who work in their school as a family. Middle school teachers may go out for a beer together and to let off steam on a Friday afternoon. Because high schools are usually larger institutions, secondary school teachers may make personal connections within a department or through participating in activities such as coaching a team or directing a play. A teacher's colleagues can become important friends and allies inside and outside the school.[2]

Just as in a family, however, tensions can develop among teachers, students, administrators, and parents. Conflict can arise from unequal power relationships within a school, differences of opinions about student behavior, a new initiative or other demand on instructional time, or competition for resources. There may be complaints about course assignments and scheduling decisions, budget allocations, choice of textbooks, or allocation of technology. Yet few schools have mechanisms built in to encourage and respond to dissident voices or opposing points of view.

Teachers have always needed a place to share ideas and let off steam. This could be one of the reasons that there are so many "parking lot conversations" after a meeting, with a range of questions and criticisms raised in the absence of the principal or department head. It can be especially difficult for a young teacher to conceive of questioning or disagreeing with an administrator. Teachers are aware that decisions about tenure (or their jobs outright, if they are in a charter school) depend on the administrator's judgment. Because school culture can seem quite intense and even incestuous at times, teachers look to friends or networks outside school for safe places to laugh, cry, vent, and get perspective and advice before returning to the workplace. And when a spouse or partner grows tired of listening to daily complaints, someone from another school may be able to empathize and provide confidential advice.

In addition to informal networks and contacts, regional and national organizations such as Facing History and Ourselves, the National School Reform Faculty, the New York Performance Standards Consortium, and the Writing Network offer opportunities for educators who share similar values or philosophies about teaching to gather. These and other networks can provide:

+ Access to a group of sympathetic peers;
+ Perspective on the adult interactions within a school;
+ Skill training, such as learning how to develop strong performance assessments or lead a Critical Friends Group;
+ Knowledge about the broader world outside one's own school;
+ New or expanded roles for teachers, including recognition as a master teacher.

Educators have found that participating in professional activities or networks *outside* the school may change their and others' perceptions of themselves and their work. Networks can offer a means of gaining recognition or earning additional certification. For example, for the past twenty-five years, accomplished teachers have been able to apply to the National Teachers Board for recognition of their instructional skills. This board certifies whether an educator has become a master teacher. The very demanding process, which requires more than a year of preparation followed by a review to determine the level of a teacher's instructional expertise, enables an outside and credible judgment of his or her standing as a professional educator.

Because working in only one school can limit teachers' understanding that schools—even those in the same school district—can function in very different ways, participation in networks can remind teachers that there is a broader world out there. Kalinda and Casey found the Brandeis/CETE monthly dinner meetings a safe place to vent about their schools. Having a confidential setting where it was safe to speak honestly about interactions at school was so important to some participants that they refused to bring colleagues from their school to the meetings! On the other hand, organizations such as the National School Reform Faculty encourage teams of teachers from various schools to attend workshops so that they can provide support to each other when they return to work.

Induction networks also provide opportunities where teachers can be tapped for leadership. In 2009–2010, the Brandeis induction program invited participants who had assumed some form of school leadership to present at two teacher leadership conferences that Brandeis organized. These conferences, which provided public acknowledgment that the presenters had become school leaders, affirmed that teachers have the ability to exercise power and should think about how to play a leading role in their schools. As Kalinda, whom we met in chapter 2, noted, "I began to think of myself as a teacher leader because you kept saying that I was one."

Some teachers are beginning to band together to create their own regional networks. Jane, a Swarthmore graduate and teacher for nine years in Philadelphia, participated in the Ford Foundation–funded Teacher Leadership for Urban Schools institutes during the summers of 2011 and 2012. These institutes affirmed Jane's ideas about the need for teachers to lead in instructional and other reforms. She reflected that "something shifted in my orientation towards my career and my work that was really important" during her time at the institute with sixteen other teacher leaders. Instead of listening to an internal voice that said, "If you're not doing something directly for the kids, you are wasting your time or not doing your job well," Jane began to envision her role as that of an inclusive teacher activist:

> There are so many things that are happening, and decisions that are being made by people who are really not informed about the context. And we are the best knowers of the context. We can be ambassadors for ourselves, for our students, for the families in our schools . . . I just feel like, my god, we really need to speak up.

After attending the first CETE summer workshop for urban teacher leaders in 2011, this very passionate urban educator decided to pursue two different objectives. First, because so many of her colleagues were discouraged because their school had been designated a school likely to close, she focused on getting recognition for two of her colleagues as outstanding teachers. This initiative was part of her desire to "find ways for teachers to become recognized as professionals," which she felt was one of the best ways to give credit to the teachers who were the heart of her school and working so hard to offer an excellent education to their students.

Jane also decided to become involved in some groups outside of her school. She noted that trying "to be a leader who does things differently, who listens and draws people out, can be really hard when you feel like you can't even get your own voice out there." Therefore, she joined with some teachers who had participated in the RESPECT Project of the U.S. Department of Education to create Teachers Lead Philly, a network focused on teacher collaboration. One of the network's first initiatives was to encourage and to help arrange visits to other teachers' classrooms. The goal was to follow the visits up with discussions about "effective instructional strategies, innovative curricula and/or meaningful assessments. We'll also develop policy guidelines that support and sustain teacher collaboration."[3] These teachers are creating ways to strengthen and share instructional strategies, partly by overcoming the isolation of teachers that makes it so challenging to share and reflect on their work.

Not only is the Philadelphia network designed to reach out horizontally to Philadelphia teachers through the Internet, Jane has also shared information about this network with her Teacher Leadership for Urban Schools institute colleagues from Boston, Providence, New Haven, and New York. She decided to find

> ways for teachers to become recognized as professionals, to be part of transforming the profession and part of the reform . . . I've got this clear sense that there's so much that is not being said that needs to be said, or it's not getting the resonance that it deserves. So, I really need to raise my status in some way, or raise my level of authority in some way, so that people take my voice a little bit more seriously, and so that I can have a bigger impact.

It is interesting that an unintended by-product of these institutes and networks is that they have also become a way to recruit teachers when there are openings in schools. As noted in the previous chapter, many teachers have become increasingly wary of transferring to other urban schools unless they know that they will be joining a group of educators who share their perspectives and values.

» ADVOCACY FOR POLICY CHANGE
Beyond the Top-Down Model

Although many teachers who participate in regional or national networks are focused on improving the instruction or the institutional functioning of their own schools, others have begun to see the need to speak up about state or federal education policies that are focused on excessive student testing, teacher accountability based on student test scores, and the unlimited growth of charter schools. They observe that educational foundations and other "reformers" have much greater access to federal and state policy makers and the media than do teachers, principals, and superintendents. There has been much more attention given to assessing oversimplified results than to building collective capacity in schools. As a result, the current top-down model focused on accountability has not provided the kind of widespread accomplishments that reformers want.

Therefore, recent education policy developments have caused teachers to question whether they can continue to keep quiet about how policy changes are affecting them and their students. Teachers used to believe that they could close their classroom doors and ignore the superintendent or the state legislator, because "this too will pass." Superintendent after superintendent would be enthusiastic about introducing new initiatives, but the teachers often became weary of the new mandated reform and would show little enthusiasm for each new district-level initiative. While that continues to be somewhat true today, state and national policies and assessments that focus on control and compliance are having an impact on classrooms and schools—especially urban and poor rural schools—that cannot be ignored. Although the past two decades of education policy initiatives have shone a well-deserved spotlight on who is not being educated well in suburban as well as urban and rural districts, and has enabled districts to begin to dismiss incompetent teachers, these policies have also had a negative impact on urban classrooms, where mandates have narrowed the curriculum and excessive time has been allocated for standardized testing (and preparing for the testing) of students. Some of the most qualified urban teachers have decided to leave the profession, which does not bode well for the direction of education in our country. As Marc Tucker, president of the National Center on Education and the Economy, notes: "It is not possible to make progress with your students if you are at war with your teachers."[4]

The model of change behind the No Child Left Behind Act and the Race to the Top initiative is a top-down model of control and compliance, or shaming, where first schools and now teachers have been labeled as failures. Some critics believe that such systemic disruption is necessary in order to make educational institutions that have been resistant to change more responsive to urban parents, who have had too few good school options for their children. They do not trust teachers, and believe that there needs to be an outside system of accountability that will make it possible to judge and label teachers as successes or failures (with numerical rankings attached). Because the authors of these reform models have ignored the voices and wisdom of practitioners (as well as factors such as poverty that have a major impact on student achievement), the seeds of failure have been sown into this top-down model.

But there is another model of accountability. Ann Cook, cochair of the New York Performance Standards Consortium,[5] offers a different model of assessment of students and teachers. Ann says that, in this model, "teachers control the rubrics; the rubrics don't control the teachers." Rather than just measuring information that students have been able to memorize, teachers in this consortium help urban students to develop a deeper understanding of the content, build analytical and other work habits, and demonstrate the skills and knowledge that they have learned. At the same time that the students are learning, teachers are developing the assessments that grow out of their teaching. As Ann Cook noted in my interview with her,

> The responsibility and the involvement of the teacher is so much greater [in this kind of teaching and assessing]. That's how you become so much more professional—by having teachers involved in the aspects of the school that create the environment, create the culture, create the specific assignments in their class . . . The bottom line for me is that, if you want kids to be more engaged [in their learning], you have to create places where adults are interacting with each other and growing professionally. Then they will be able to reach out and engage kids.

The members of the New York Performance Standards Consortium believe strongly that *both* teachers and students should be responsible for demonstrating what they have accomplished. This belief is based on an understanding that such assessment should be part of a process of learning and revision on the part of both the students and teachers.

Thus, we have two different visions of teaching and accountability: one where teachers are professionals trusted to be part of the creation of teacher-designed assessments, with the results examined with colleagues so that the teachers can reflect together about how to teach effectively. In the other, more widespread approach in today's schools, teachers are assessed and ranked by their students' "value added" scores on standardized tests created by publishers.

The increased antagonism toward and scapegoating of teachers has motivated some educators to move into the policy arena. They have begun to realize that they could learn from the example of some organizations, such as Teach for America (TFA), that have been invited to policy discussions. TFA, whose philosophy follows a "Teaching as Leadership" framework, recruits university students graduating in the top of their classes to teach for two years in urban schools as the way to address the "social justice challenge of this generation." The organization's goal is that, after teaching for two years, TFA alumni will proceed to have an impact on education policy as a result of their experiences. Many TFA alumni have moved on to policy arenas and are now working in the U.S. Department of Education or serving in the U.S. Senate and in state departments of education.

TFA is strongly associated with educational "entrepreneurs" who advocate for enlarging TFA partnerships with urban school districts (and hiring TFA to replace more experienced teachers), removing caps on charter schools (regardless of how poorly they are educating their students), closing "failing schools," and increasing competition for resources among traditional and charter schools as a means of improving teaching and learning. This policy agenda, which has been embraced by many Republicans and Democrats, has shifted the responsibility for overcoming the effects of poverty on children solely onto the shoulders of the teachers in what has been called a "no excuses" philosophy.

There are other education groups advocating for different goals and roles than those espoused by the "reformers" creating the policy agendas today. For example, Richard Rothstein and the Broader, Bolder Approach to Education organization assert that if we intend to narrow or eliminate the achievement gap, in addition to strong teachers, state and federal governments must support universal early childhood education, wrap-around health services, and other antipoverty initiatives such as improving available jobs and housing.[6] The Forum for Education and Democracy,[7] an organization founded by Debbie Meier and educators who have worked on the Essential Schools that Ted and Nancy Sizer founded, also offers a different vision of educational change than the one being promoted by the reformers in power in state and federal governments. With the exception of Diane Ravitch's,[8] however, few of these voices are being heard in today's media and policy arena.

In such a policy setting, where teachers believe that policy makers are not paying attention to their needs and concerns, many teachers are uncertain about how to be heard. Ann Cook notes that most teachers want to be seen as professionals and not someone on a picket line. "If you say the word 'politics' to them, they're going to run the other way." Many teachers also feel as though they don't have the expertise to speak up in the policy arena. As a result, some organizations have sprung up to encourage or facilitate teacher voices. Celine Coggins founded Teach Plus, an advocacy organization that encourages teachers in various cities to apply to join a cohort that reflects on policy issues, learns to write op-ed pieces, lobbies for legislation, and communicates with superintendents of schools. (It was a group of Teach Plus teachers that developed the idea for Teacher Turnaround Teams [T3], the reform model discussed in chapter 5.) As of 2013, there are Teach Plus sites in Boston, Chicago, Indianapolis, Los Angeles, Memphis, and Washington, DC, where teachers are encouraged to contribute their voices in the policy arena.

The Center for Teaching Quality (CTQ),[9] founded by Barnett Berry, also affirms teaching as a profession and the need for teacher leadership by experienced teachers. In January 2010, Barnett Berry, Alesha Daughtrey, and Alan Wieder wrote that their research indicated that "teachers who report more control over the policies in their schools and greater degrees of autonomy in their jobs are more likely to remain in teaching and to feel invested in their careers and schools." Berry has created the Teacher Leaders Network, a virtual community "by which teacher leadership can be nurtured and expertise can be spread," because:

+ Teacher leadership is a critical component of effective teaching and school success.
+ Accomplished teachers tend to seek out leadership opportunities but require support to fulfill their promise as leaders.
+ Expanding leadership roles and advancement opportunities for teachers may be an excellent and cost-effective strategy for retaining the most effective teachers.[10]

» AMPLIFYING EDUCATORS' VOICES
New Avenues for Change

In addition to giving more responsibility (and authority to make changes) to teacher leaders within schools, I believe that we also should rethink how education policy is defined and implemented in this country. We need to find different ways and models to involve the voices of educators and to listen to the recommendations of the educational professionals who are expected to implement desired changes.

This will not be easy. Hierarchical structures within schools and districts discourage teachers from thinking that they have a valid role in policy making. Bureaucrats in state and federal governments seem far removed from the process of education, and they do not appear interested in teachers' perceptions. Most individual teachers have not felt that they have the credibility or authority to challenge this structure. Even thinking about challenging the hierarchy seems quite removed from the lives and work of most teachers. This is why the work of the Center for Teaching Quality is important as a way to give some teachers a forum and the skills and confidence to express their opinions.

As the focus of reform moves to teacher evaluation, pay, and tenure, more and more teachers may feel that they have no choice but to become involved. The question then becomes: what avenues are available to teachers to develop and express their opinions on education policy issues? The traditional avenue would be through the teacher unions, which historically have represented teachers' interests by negotiating working conditions, including evaluations. Yet it is not so obvious whether unions will be the leading venue to represent the range of teachers' concerns about education policy and reform. Education Sector researchers Sarah Rosenberg and Elena Silva, with the Farkas Duffett Research (FDR) Group, in a report on teacher unions and the future of the profession, write:

> Today's teachers want more than just bread-and-butter basics from their unions. They expect that unions will not only protect them, but also will engage in some of the reforms aimed at transforming their profession … Still, for some teachers, the union's role should be to stand against

the rising tide of reform. "If they're raising requirements, because they're always raising requirements on what teachers have to do, somebody's job needs to be 'no.'"[11]

Unions themselves face challenges both internally and externally. Mark Teoh and Celine Coggins, researchers at Teach Plus, point out that teachers with fewer than ten years and those with more than eleven years disagree on some key policy issues.[12] Teachers with less experience think that student learning growth measured through standardized assessments should represent 20 percent or more of teacher evaluations. They also express interest in establishing varying salaries based on student outcomes, as opposed to awarding higher salaries based on seniority. Teachers with eleven or more years' experience oppose these policies. Beginning and veteran teachers thus appear to want conflicting things from their unions. Although both groups of teachers agree that providing teachers more time to collaborate with peers is necessary to improve student achievement, union leaders would be hard pressed to develop reform policies about evaluation and compensation that would unify these members. (There might also be a lag in which policies the unions would support, since it is usually veteran teachers who control the leadership of a union.)

To complicate things even more, unions themselves are engaged in a struggle for survival in some states. In Wisconsin and Michigan, Republican governors have moved to limit the unions' power, and governors in some other states are exploring doing the same. Therefore, some unions find themselves fighting a battle for survival rather than leading the effort to envision and negotiate school reform.

Even if the younger teachers had a stronger identification with union goals, however, it appears that only a small percentage is interested in participating in union organizations. What does attract more of the younger teachers is the chance to express their opinions through networks and blogs. Technology gives them the space to find others who might share their opinions. Listservers and blogs offer the safety of anonymity in reading different opinions before deciding to venture into policy discussions. (In some ways, this is not so different from the large number of teachers who used to attend union meetings, listen, and vote without venturing to express their opinions at microphones. I remember how much courage it took to speak at the microphone at a Boston Teachers Union meeting.)

Not only do teachers find strength in numbers when they communicate with colleagues at Teachers Lead Philly or Teach Plus, but the reassuring give-and-take found through horizontal communication enables participants to engage and improve their ideas with others before expressing them as their own opinions.[13] And because most educational networks such as the Center for Teaching Quality or the Forum for Education and Democracy operate outside of schools, a teacher may become quite involved in policy or instructional deliberations without being identified or singled out in his or her school. Thus, being part of a horizontal group of teachers does not require that a teacher or small group of teachers stand up inside a school or district to challenge those in authority who are proposing policies; instead, they can be part of a larger number protesting these policies online. Moreover, social media do have the potential to develop innovative ways to record what kind of impact policies are having in schools.

Technology and networks are beginning to offer new ways to develop models to involve educators not only in responding to education policies, but also in developing, implementing, and evaluating different models of educational practice and policy. For example, Mehta, Gomez, and Bryk, in an essay in *The Futures of School Reform*, argue that the entire hierarchical policy development model needs to be rethought. Dismissing the current model as left over from an industrial, hierarchical age, they advocate developing Networked Improvement Communities (NICs) of educators to "spur social learning and innovation."[14] Multiple schools or districts would choose to participate in the educational NICs that would develop:

- Common targets with measurable and ambitious (but feasible) goals;
- A shared language community around an explicitly mapped, complex problem space;
- A continuous improvement ethic undergirded by an agreed-upon and rigorous set of inquiry methods.[15]

The authors envision that teachers and principals would be involved in analyzing and developing solutions to instructional and institutional dilemmas: examining and sharing what works, what fails, and why. Each NIC would agree to tackle a significant challenge of practice, such as who drops or is pushed out of school and what can be done to change this. In an NIC, different schools would each agree to work on one aspect of this problem, "with one group of schools seeking to foster better relationships with adults, another seeking to build students' academic skills, and a third working with community agencies to combat local gangs. Over time, what is learned on each of these fronts would be integrated into a more systemic approach."[16] After the network has developed a range of solutions, educators would select the one that was the best fit with their own school context.

Although this proposed model is quite new and experimental, it intrigues me, because the authors conceive of teachers as professionals who are central to defining the problems, considering and trying out potential solutions, and then using their professional judgment to decide which researched solutions would work best in their school's context. The authors understand that teacher leaders must contribute to and be deeply connected to the evolving shared professional knowledge about practice and policy. They also are trying to create a third space for policy development and implementation, outside the very polarized education policy debates raging in states and on the federal level.

In 1974, David Tyack wrote about education reformers who were looking for the "one best system."[17] Tyack noted that there was never one simple, true answer to solve complicated educational problems. We can see that some of that hope for one true answer has survived until today, because education reformers insist that if we could just weaken or eliminate unions and their resistance to changing working conditions and seniority, and create as many charter schools as possible (end the "public school monopoly"), we would be able to reform our urban schools. In some ways, today's debates about education reform echo the polarized politicians' debates—the focus is on oversimplifying the challenges while demonizing opponents. While such negative campaigns may be effective in hurting the image of the opponents (e.g., the public is losing faith in teachers in general), they do little to advance effective solutions to the very complicated problems that continue to challenge educators, students, parents, and communities.

Real solutions will not arise from outsiders mandating simplistic solutions such as removing the cap on all charter schools, no matter how effective they may be in doing that. Nor are politicians likely to agree to let educators create all of their own assessments. Because we need more nuanced education policy that recognizes the complexity of teaching and of improving schools, it is essential that we find ways to listen to the voices of those who live and understand the day-to-day challenges of educating all students. We must be willing to give educators agency, take some risks, and leverage whatever incremental changes make sense rather than waiting for full-scale change before addressing specific instructional and institutional challenges. Those inside and outside of schools have to work together to analyze educational problems and policies, and to assess the strengths and weaknesses of each potential option or solution, if we want to effect lasting change that will make positive differences in the lives of students and teachers.

If you want to improve the quality of teaching and learning, you must develop the capacity of teachers. Are teachers the problem or the solution? The answer is "yes." Yes, teachers are the problem, because they are ultimately responsible (along with parents and students) for our present shortcomings. And yes, they are the solution, because they are the people who must act if there is to be a solution at all.

—THOMAS SOBOL[1]

CONCLUSION

One Classroom, One School, and One Network at a Time

THIS BOOK HAS FOCUSED on the importance of teacher leadership within classrooms and schools as well as in networks for sharing ideas outside school. The teachers and principals portrayed in this book are committed to working with each other to improve their professional learning communities. They believe that we must pay much more attention to what is going on in the "black box" that is the school, and acknowledge that:

- In order to be effective instructional and school leaders, teachers need to learn skills about working with colleagues.
- The principal's leadership has a critical impact on school culture, including whether teacher leadership is welcomed or discouraged.

+ Because of differences among classrooms in any one school and among various schools in a district, one size of reform for all schools does not work.

Narrow test-driven reforms have not been effective in reducing the achievement gap nor in helping American students to do better on international assessments, especially on tests that require critical thinking or problem solving. We will not be able to educate all of our children so that they become productive citizens in our democracy unless passionate and smart teachers in our schools gain more agency and power to solve problems.

Professionals in the field of education make the difference as to whether an education reform or initiative succeeds or fails. It is imperative that policy makers and reformers seek their guidance as we proceed. We need to identify and support teacher leaders whose knowledge and skills about working with others, passion for reform, and willingness to take risks have made significant contributions to their schools. If these are the kinds of educator-professionals we want *and* need, it makes sense to look backward to see how to develop such teacher leaders. In the stories and voices of the educators described in this book, we can, first, find some common themes, and then define steps to develop and support teacher leaders.

TEACHER LEADERS ARE MADE, NOT BORN

The stories in this book indicate that teacher leaders have emerged from different teacher education programs—both traditional and alternative. (It is noteworthy, however, that many graduates of the teacher preparation programs at Consortium for Excellence in Teacher Education (CETE) colleges and universities, with their emphasis on the big picture outside of the classroom and on critical thinking and inquiry, do become teacher leaders.) The teacher stories in this book acknowledge that some potential teacher leaders self-identify; many others are tapped by mentors. It is helpful for teachers to be able to explore various leadership opportunities, such as engaging in action research, where they can reflect with colleagues about their frustrations and accomplishments.

What makes some teachers decide to go on to work more visibly with others to change curriculum, instruction, or the way that a school functions? The data in this book are anecdotal, but they provide some indicators about which educators develop a sense of agency that enables them to find their voices as leaders. First, prospective teacher leaders must be respected as strong classroom teachers, regardless of the school setting. Some decide to share what they have developed in their classrooms as they engage in reflective dialogues within a Critical Friends Group or some other kind of adult learning community. Others become motivated to speak up because of ethical concerns about how some students, peers, or community members are being treated in a school. A third impetus can be found in teachers' growing frustration about the dissonance between mandated education policies and the complicated realities teachers face each day in their schools. While most teacher leaders choose to work with colleagues on instructional issues, others feel drawn to improving how the school as an institution affects students and/or adults. And some teacher leaders feel more comfortable participating as part of a network outside their school.

Those interested in encouraging teacher leadership need to recognize that educators may be ready to assume significant leadership responsibilities at different times in their careers. The traditional route is for second-stage teachers to assume leadership after they have mastered the beginning challenges of teaching. As we have read, however, that is not the reality for young teachers in charter and small urban secondary schools. Some new teachers hit the ground running in these schools, responding to the expectation that they will take on leadership roles in addition to teaching very long hours. Leaders in these small urban schools need to realize that, while these beginning teachers may be very excited about these opportunities, they will also need mentoring and support as they struggle to learn to teach and lead at the same time.

TEACHER LEADERS NEED TO DEVELOP NEW SKILLS

As Casey indicated in chapter 2, we have to change the culture for the adults in a school if we want to change the culture for kids. If American graduates need to be able to solve problems, work well with others, demonstrate creativity, and make critical decisions, their teachers must first model these skills.

Working with adults is not the same as teaching students. Whether they want to work in the instructional or the institutional arena, teacher leaders must learn organizational and political skills. They need to become institutionally and culturally competent, which involves learning how to build on social and professional capital within the school. A teacher who wants to exercise leadership should eventually be able to maneuver through relationships with peers and supervisors, gain allies, and acknowledge those who are perceived to be powerful, while still moving forward to make change happen. As we have read, teacher leaders need to know how to:

+ Decide which short-term and long-term battles to undertake or decline;
+ Gain allies and develop relational trust among different constituencies;
+ Persist in working toward a goal despite any pushback about personal motives;
+ Not take opposition personally.

They should also learn that they themselves have some power, and then decide when and how they want to exercise that power.

EFFECTIVE TEACHER LEADERSHIP REQUIRES FLEXIBLE SUPPORTS

Good mentoring for teacher leaders helps them gain the human resources and political skills needed for working with adult colleagues. Mentoring can make the difference in whether a teacher leader learns to recover from mistakes made while becoming a leader, or considers herself as someone who has failed and then retreats from leadership challenges. Mentors can also advise their colleagues about which tasks they should and should not take on in their beginning years of teaching, as we observed in the mentoring Michael received and the lack of mentoring that Kelsey experienced.

Those interested in developing teacher leaders must learn to recognize various groups' needs and interests. One of the challenges facing educators is how to improve the work/life balance for talented teachers at various stages of their lives and careers. Whether they are teaching in urban or suburban schools, fewer young people today expect to remain in teaching as a lifelong career. Thus, teachers in charter and small urban schools, who are typically asked to step up to leadership roles even as they are learning how to teach, may not worry about whether they can sustain such work beyond the next year or so. On the other hand, teacher leadership roles can also be very attractive to second-stage teachers who are comfortable in the classroom and are looking for new challenges.

Women and people of color can face some unique challenges in becoming leaders. Although they may have developed the ability to navigate well among people, some of these educators internalize criticism that arises from peers or supervisors. Or they may be especially surprised by a lack of support from their peers. Such negative feedback can immobilize them, and they may decide that they do not want to be visible leaders. As Lee pointed out in chapter three, "Honestly, I like to be liked, and you don't always get to be liked when you're the one in charge." When teacher leaders are weighing whether or not to continue, principals and mentors need to point out how their leadership is making a difference in children's learning.

Most of the secondary school teacher leaders interviewed for this book held informal or semiformal leadership positions. This arrangement had the advantage of allowing these educators to move back and forth between the classroom and other roles in the school—sometimes emphasizing their leadership tasks, at other times focusing more on their classroom work or on their families. Flexibility made it possible for these educators to try out leadership in more limited ways, without making a decision about moving out of the classroom. At the same time, because the leadership tasks were on top of their full-time, challenging teaching responsibilities, these educators often ended up feeling drained and reluctant to volunteer again.

THE PRINCIPAL'S COMMITMENT IS KEY

If teacher leadership is to become part of greater organizational change, a principal must establish a culture where teachers can innovate within a system of mutual accountability. Relationships among the adults are key to effective institutional leadership. Knowing that there may be pressure from colleagues that discourages a teacher from standing out, a principal must affirm and implement a transparent process to select teacher leaders. Teacher leaders report that they would like principals to:

+ Focus on establishing relational trust among all who work, learn, and lead in the school;
+ Encourage a teacher to explore different leadership opportunities that may match his or her own style and strength;
+ Make teacher leadership a personal priority, or establish at least one person with power and resources for whom it is a significant priority to develop and mentor teacher leaders;
+ Help teachers learn how to be visible and to function effectively in a political environment;
+ Provide mentors and establish conditions under which teachers can participate in an initiative, make some mistakes without too high a cost, and gradually learn how to assume responsibility and power;
+ Create incentives for teachers to assume leadership roles.

Teaching is incredibly hard work. To expect that teachers can add significant leadership responsibilities to their workload without in some way modifying their other responsibilities is not a workable model. While some second-stage teachers welcome new responsibilities when they begin to "plateau," they also report that they are searching for time to do everything well. They need a partial release from their teaching load in order to be able to sustain these leadership roles. Developing more formal roles in secondary schools could also enable teachers to feel that they have sanctioned as well as informal authority to make suggestions and plans.

Schools will have the benefit of more teacher leaders if we begin to find, develop, and support principals who are prepared to make teacher leadership a reality. While I acknowledge that a principal will undoubtedly face challenges in encouraging and institutionalizing teacher leadership, it is possible that many more would undertake these challenges if principals were all held accountable for identifying and supporting teacher leaders.

TEACHER LEADERSHIP REQUIRES A CULTURE OF TRUST

Teacher leaders cannot change the culture of a school by themselves; they need the cooperation of others. Principals and mentors should have clear expectations for the teacher leader and how he or she fits into a school initiative. Teacher leaders should be given tasks that are attainable; they need help defining the scope of a problem so they can develop strategies for realizing short-term and long-term goals.

Principals need to develop systemic ways that teachers' voices can be heard, and to encourage expression of divergent opinions while plans are being made, rather than driving them underground or to the parking lot. A principal should understand that lack of disagreement in a conversation or meeting may reflect compliance rather than consensus. Unless principals learn how to hear teachers' questions and quiet concerns, they will not be able to anticipate opposition and implementation problems that may arise. Smart principals will look to their teacher leaders as critical allies who can contribute experience and wisdom as the professional school team works together to improve teaching and learning and the institutional culture.

Teachers need feedback and support that enable them to learn from their successes and mistakes and to make adjustments en route. They also must have power to carry out their responsibilities. It is extremely frustrating to do the work and then be undercut at the end of the process. This would argue for principals to establish a process where teacher leaders, mentors, and the principal check in with each other while defining the problem, developing possible solutions, and considering intended and unintended consequences. When teacher conversation and advice can move safely into the public arena (instead of being given behind the scenes), the school develops a much healthier culture. Everyone benefits from hearing different points of view, as long as the dialogue is part of a structured process that enables decisions to be made and implemented.

TEACHER LEADERS CAN BUILD CAPACITY
FOR SUSTAINED REFORM

Education reformers express frustration with incremental change, but the sweeping changes mandated by the No Child Left Behind Act and the Race to the Top initiative have not proven to be effective in significantly narrowing the achievement gap. Instead, they have demoralized teachers, who are now being blamed for the failures of these policies.

What has proved effective, however, is building capacity among educators who work together to implement a shared vision of reform. We will only be able to improve the schools significantly when we strengthen educators' knowledge, skills, dispositions, and their ability to work with others. Teachers must be key players in accomplishing instructional and institutional change.

As Richard Elmore reminds us, the enduring challenge continues to be how to reproduce what works in one classroom or school and scale up the reform so that more schools and districts can improve at the same time.[2] Because such change is needed in many schools and districts, it is worthwhile to consider models that have the potential to affect districts and networks of schools as well as individual schools. The models for teacher leadership presented in chapter 5 affirm the importance of teacher leaders' experience, professional knowledge, and collaboration. This recognition of the need for training teacher leaders has also been affirmed by the Partnerships to Uplift Communities (PUC) and KIPP (Knowledge Is Power Program) charter school networks, which are devoting time and resources to recruiting talented teachers and having them learn from each other what has worked for educators in successful schools.

Some reformers are considering how to reconfigure the basic structure of schools and how they currently function. It will be useful to reflect on teacher leader roles as the field pilots new school models. Whether the model envisioned for Networked Improvement Communities (NICs) is implemented, or reformers develop some other version, Mehta, Gomez, and Bryk note that practitioners interested in change must be involved throughout the process of reform to:[3]

+ Define the complex and interrelated aspects of the educational challenges;
+ Help to identify how various options might work differently in different school contexts and then to implement these options under realistic conditions;
+ Work with others to assess and evaluate what is effective in different school contexts;
+ Disseminate potential solutions, recognizing that professional educators will need to make decisions about which solutions work in their school.

None of the teacher leadership models described in this book depends on a heroic single educator to reform a school. Neither the principal nor teacher leaders are expected to do the work by themselves. We have read that teacher networks and regional groups offer educators a safe place outside their school where they can reflect on what is occurring in the workplace. Educators need a place where they can laugh, cry, and get intellectual nourishment and renewed energy to go back into the arena again.

As Berg and Souvanna report, unless schools are structured to welcome and sustain teacher leadership, even teacher leaders who are well trained will not remain in those roles.[4] Rather, they will want to leave the schools (and perhaps the profession) if their work is ignored or undercut. There are also questions about sustainability and how reform initiatives will be institutionalized once initial funding and support ends. If we are to learn from past failures to mandate reforms, teacher leaders must be a central part of the deliberative process where they can contribute their professional judgment (based on research and the specific context of their schools and classrooms) about proposed school reforms.

It is time to end the blame and shame focused on teachers. Success depends instead on identifying, developing, and supporting teacher leaders who will work with colleagues and principals to:

+ Solve challenging educational dilemmas of how to engage and motivate diverse students so that they can attain their potential; and

+ Reach out to the community and nonprofit agencies to work together to alleviate the impact of poverty so that all children are prepared to learn.

This is hard work. It will not be accomplished in a year or two, but it can and must be done. Students, communities, and our country will benefit from the leadership of strong principals and teacher leaders whose knowledge, experience, dedication, and passion provide the basis for improving our schools.

NOTES

CHAPTER 1

1. Teacher Leadership Exploratory Consortium, "Teacher Leader Model Standards," www.teacherleaderstandards.org/downloads/TLS_Brochure.pdf.

2. Kevin Costante, "Leading the Instructional Core: An Interview with Richard Elmore," *In Conversation* 11, no. 3 (2010): 1–12, www.edu.gov.on.ca/eng/policyfunding/leadership/summer2010.pdf.

3. Susan Moore Johnson and Morgaen L. Donaldson, "Overcoming Obstacles to Leadership," *Educational Leadership* 65, no. 1 (2007): 8–13.

4. Sharon Feiman-Nemser, "From Preparation to Practice: Designing a Continuum to Strengthen and Sustain Teaching," *Teachers College Record* 103, no. 6 (2003): 1013–1055.

5. Richard Elmore, foreword to *The Power of Teacher Teams*, by Vivian Troen and Katherine C. Boles (Thousand Oaks, CA: Corwin Press, 2012), xv.

6. Anthony S. Bryk and Barbara Schneider, *Trust in Schools: A Core Resource for Improvement* (New York: Russell Sage Foundation, 2002).

7. Ann Lieberman and Lynne Miller, *Teacher Leadership* (San Francisco: Jossey-Bass, 2004), 28–29.

8. National School Reform Faculty, Harmony Education Center, 8/13/2012, www.nsrfharmony.org/faq.html.

9. Dan Lortie, *Schoolteacher: A Sociological Study* (Chicago: University of Chicago Press, 1975).

10. Johnson and Donaldson, "Overcoming Obstacles to Leadership," 10.

11. Bryk and Schneider, *Trust in Schools*.

12. Lieberman and Miller, *Teacher Leadership*, 39.

CHAPTER 2

1. Judith Warren Little, "Assessing the Prospects for Teacher Leadership," in *Building a Professional Culture in Schools*, ed. Ann Lieberman (New York: Teachers College Press, 1988), 100.

2. M. Katzenmeyer and G. Moller, *Awakening the Sleeping Giant: Helping Teachers Develop as Leaders* (Thousand Oaks, CA: Corwin Press, 2009), 32.

3. Katherine K. Merseth et al., *Inside Urban Charter Schools: Promising Practices and Strategies in Five High-Performing Schools* (Cambridge, MA: Harvard Education Press, 2009), 160.

CHAPTER 3

1. Interview with a teacher who had worked in a Washington, DC, charter school.

2. The author heard these comments in a workshop in 1981.

3. Lois P. Frankel, *Nice Girls Don't Get the Corner Office: 101 Unconscious Mistakes Women Make That Sabotage Their Careers* (New York: Warner Business Books, 2004), 24–27.

4. Andy Hargreaves and Michael Fullan, *Professional Capital: Transforming Teaching in Every School* (New York: Teachers College Press, 2012), 90.

5. Heather G. Peske et al., "The Next Generation of Teachers: Changing Conceptions of a Career in Teaching," *Phi Delta Kappan* 83, no. 4 (2001): 304–311.

6. Charles Taylor Kerchner with Laura Steen Mulfinger, "Can Teachers Run Their Own Schools? Tales from the Islands of Teacher Cooperatives," October 2010, http://www.charlestkerchner.com/cr/uploadImages/Teacher_run_case.pdf, 22.

CHAPTER 4

1. Larry Cuban, *Inside the Black Box of Classroom Practice: Change Without Reform in American Education* (Cambridge, MA: Harvard Education Press, 2013).

2. Andy Hargreaves and Michael Fullan, *Professional Capital: Transforming Teaching in Every School* (New York: Teachers College Press, 2012), 87.

3. Anthony S. Bryk and Barbara Schneider, *Trust in Schools: A Core Resource for Improvement* (New York: Russell Sage Foundation, 2002).

4. Review on *Insideschools* website, a project of the Center for New York City Affairs at The New School, accessed October 5, 2012, http://www.insideschool.org.

5. Charles Taylor Kerchner with Laura Steen Mulfinger, "Can Teachers Run Their Own Schools? Tales from the Islands of Teacher Cooperatives," October 2010, http://www.charlestkerchner.com/cr/uploadImages/Teacher_run_case.pdf, 23.

CHAPTER 5

1. Jill Harrison Berg and Phomdaen Souvanna, "The Boston Teacher Leadership Certificate Program: Building Resources for Reform" (paper presented at the annual meeting of the American Educational Research Association, Vancouver, British Columbia, Canada, April 17, 2012), 41.

2. Charles Taylor Kerchner with Laura Steen Mulfinger, "Can Teachers Run Their Own Schools? Tales from the Islands of Teacher Cooperatives," October 2010, http://www.charlestkerchner.com/cr/uploadImages/Teacher_run_case.pdf, 17.

3. Ronald A. Heifetz and Marty Linsky, *Leadership on the Line: Staying Alive Through the Dangers of Leading* (Boston, MA: Harvard Business School Press, 2002).

4. Teach Plus, *Ready for the Next Challenge: Improving the Retention and Distribution of Excellent Teachers in Urban Schools* (Cambridge, MA: Teach Plus, 2009).

5. Teach Plus, "Our Mission," "Why We Exist," http://www.teachplus.org/page/history-and-mission-62.html.

6. Kristen Ferris, "Human Capital in Turnaround Schools," *School Administrator* 69, no. 7 (2012): 36–39.

7. Susan Moore Johnson, Matthew A. Kraft, and John P. Papay, "How Context Matters in High-Need Schools: The Effects of Teachers' Working Conditions on Their Professional Satisfaction and Their Students' Achievement," *Teachers College Record* 114, no. 10 (2012): 2.

8. Aspen Institute and Annenberg Institute for School Reform, *Strong Foundation, Evolving Challenges: A Case Study to Support Leadership Transition in the Boston Public Schools*, March 2006, http://annenberginstitute.org/sites/default/files/product/250/files/Boston-CaseStudy.pdf, 6.

9. Berg et al., "The Boston Teacher Leadership Certificate Program," 9.

10. Ibid., 41.

11. Johnson et al., "How Context Matters in High-Need Schools," 16.

CHAPTER 6

1. Teacher Leadership Exploratory Consortium, "Teacher Leader Model Standards," www.teacherleaderstandards.org/the_standards_domain_7.

2. Carrie R. Leana, "The Missing Link in School Reform," *Stanford Social Innovation Review*, Fall 2011, http://ssireview.org/articles/entry/the_missing_link_in_school_reform.

3. Teachers Lead Philly, "Projects: Themes: 2012–2013, Effective Teacher Collaboration," September 7, 2012, www.teachersleadphilly.org/projects.html.

4. Joe Nocera, "How to Fix the Schools," *New York Times*, September 17, 2012.

5. New York Performance Standards Consortium, http://performanceassessment.org.

6. See http://www.boldapproach.org.

7. See http://forumforeducation.org.

8. Diane Ravitch, *The Death and Life of the Great American School System: How Testing and Choice Are Undermining Education* (New York: Basic Books, 2011).

9. See http://www.teachingquality.org.

10. Barnett Berry, Alesha Daughtrey, and Alan Wieder, *Teacher Leadership: Leading the Way to Effective Teaching and Learning* (Hillsborough, NC: Center for Teaching Quality, 2010), 9.

11. Sarah Rosenberg and Elena Silva with the FDR Group, *Trending Toward Reform: Teachers Speak on Unions and the Future of the Profession* (Washington, DC: Education Sector, 2012), 3.

12. Mark Teoh and Celine Coggins, *Great Expectations: Teachers' Views on Elevating the Teaching Profession* (Boston: Teach Plus, 2012).

13. Leana, "The Missing Link in School Reform."

14. Jal Mehta, Louis M. Gomez, and Anthony S. Bryk, "Building on Practical Knowledge: The Key to a Stronger Profession Is Learning from the Field," in *The Futures of School Reform*, eds. Jal Mehta, Robert B. Schwartz, and Frederick M. Hess (Cambridge, MA: Harvard Education Press, 2012), 45.

15. Ibid., 47.

16. Ibid., 49.

17. 7. David Tyack, *The One Best System: A History of American Urban Education* (Cambridge, MA: Harvard University Press, 1974.)

CONCLUSION

1. Thomas Sobol, *My Life in School* (New York: Public Schools for Tomorrow, 2013), 165.

2. Richard Elmore, "Getting to Scale with Good Educational Practice," *Harvard Educational Review* 66, no. 1 (Spring 1996): 1–26.

3. Jal Mehta, Louis M. Gomez, and Anthony S. Bryk, "Building on Practical Knowledge: The Key to a Stronger Profession Is Learning from the Field," in *The Futures of School Reform*, eds. Jal Mehta, Robert B. Schwartz, and Frederick M. Hess (Cambridge, MA: Harvard Education Press, 2012).

4. Jill Harrison Berg and Phomdaen Souvanna, "The Boston Teacher Leadership Certificate Program: Building Resources for Reform" (paper presented at the annual meeting of the American Educational Research Association, Vancouver, British Columbia, Canada, April 17, 2012), 41.

ADDITIONAL READING

Ackerman, Richard H., and Sarah V. Mackenzie, eds. *Uncovering Teacher Leadership: Essays and Voices from the Field*. Thousand Oaks, CA: Corwin Press, 2007.

Barth, Roland S. *Improving Schools from Within*. San Francisco: Jossey-Bass, 1991.

Berry, Barnett, Alesha Daughtrey, and Alan Wieder. *Teacher Leadership: Leading the Way to Effective Teaching and Learning*. Hillsborough, NC: Center for Teaching Quality, 2010.

Bryk, Anthony S., and Barbara Schneider. *Trust in Schools: A Core Resource for Improvement*. New York: The Russell Sage Foundation, 2002.

Bryk, Anthony S. et al. *Organizing Schools for Improvement: Lessons from Chicago*. Chicago: University of Chicago Press, 2010.

Chauncey, Caroline, ed. *Strategic Priorities for School Improvement*. Cambridge, MA: Harvard Education Press, 2010.

Christensen, Clayton M., Michael B. Horn, and Curtis W. Johnson. *Disrupting Class: How Disruptive Innovation Will Change the Way the World Learns*. New York: McGraw Hill, 2008.

Cochran-Smith, Marilyn, and Susan L. Lytle. *Inquiry as Stance: Practitioner Research for the Next Generation*. New York: Teachers College Press, 2009.

Cohen, David K. *Teaching and Its Predicaments*. Cambridge, MA: Harvard University Press, 2011.

Crowther, Frank, with Margaret Ferguson and Leonne Hann. *Developing Teacher Leaders: How Teacher Leadership Enhances School Success*. Thousand Oaks, CA: Corwin Press, 2009.

Cuban, Larry. *Inside the Black Box of Classroom Practice: Change without Reform in American Education*. Cambridge, MA: Harvard Education Press, 2013.

Danielson, Charlotte. *Teacher Leadership That Strengthens Professional Practice*. Alexandria, VA: Association for Supervision and Curriculum Development, 2006.

Darling-Hammond, Linda, and Joan Baratz-Snowden, eds. *A Good Teacher in Every Classroom: Preparing the Highly Qualified Teachers Our Children Deserve*. San Francisco: Jossey-Bass, 2005.

Elmore, Richard. *Building a New Structure for School Improvement*. Washington, DC: The Albert Shanker Institute, 2000.

———. *School Reform from the Inside Out: Policy, Practice, and Performance*. Cambridge, MA: Harvard Education Press, 2006.

———. Foreword in *The Power of Teacher Teams*, edited by Vivian Troen and Katherine C. Boles. Thousand Oaks, CA: Corwin Press, 2012.

Farr, Stephen. *Teaching as Leadership: The Highly Effective Teacher's Guide to Closing the Achievement Gap.* San Francisco: Jossey-Bass, 2010.

Feiman-Nemser, Sharon. *Teachers as Learners.* Cambridge, MA: Harvard Education Press, 2012.

Hargreaves, Andy, and Michael Fullan. *Professional Capital: Transforming Teaching in Every School.* New York: Teachers College Press, 2012.

Heifetz, Ronald A. *Leadership Without Easy Answers.* Cambridge, MA: The Belknap Press of Harvard University Press, 1994.

Heifetz, Ronald A., and Marty Linsky. *Leadership on the Line: Staying Alive Through the Dangers of Leading.* Boston, MA: Harvard Business School Press, 2002.

Johnson, Susan Moore, and Morgaen L. Donaldson. "Overcoming the Obstacles to Leadership." *Educational Leadership* 59, no. 6 (2007): 12–16.

Johnson, Susan Moore, Matthew A. Kraft, and John P. Papay, "How Context Matters in High-Need Schools: The Effects of Teachers' Working Conditions on Their Professional Satisfaction and Their Students' Achievement." *Teachers College Record* 114, no. 10 (2012): 2.

Johnson, Susan Moore, and The Project on the Next Generation of Teachers. *Finders and Keepers: Helping New Teachers Survive and Thrive in Our Schools.* San Francisco: Jossey-Bass, 2004.

Katzenmeyer, Marilyn, and Gayle Moller. *Awakening the Sleeping Giant: Helping Teachers Develop as Leaders.* Thousand Oaks, CA: Corwin Press, 2009.

Lampert, Linda. *Building Leadership Capacity in Schools.* Alexandria, VA: Association for Supervision and Curriculum Development, 1998.

Lieberman, Ann, and Linda D. Friedrich. *How Teachers Become Leaders: Learning from Practice and Research.* New York: Teachers College Press, 2010.

Lieberman, Ann, and Lynne Miller. *Teacher Leadership.* San Francisco: Jossey-Bass, 2004.

Lieberman, Ann, Ellen R. Saxl, and Matthew B. Miles. "Teacher Leadership: Ideology and Practice," in *Building a Professional Culture in School,* edited by Ann Lieberman, 148–166. New York: Teachers College Press, 1988.

Little, Judith Warren. "Assessing the Prospects for Teacher Leadership," in *Building a Professional Culture in School,* edited by Ann Lieberman. New York: Teachers College Press, 1988.

———. "The Persistence of Privacy: Autonomy and Initiative in Teachers' Professional Relations." *Teachers College Record* 91, no. 4 (1990): 509–536.

Lortie, Dan C. *Schoolteacher: A Sociological Study.* Chicago: University of Chicago Press, 1975.

Maxfield, Charles R., and Shannon Flumerfelt. "The Empowering Principal: Leadership Behaviors Needed by Effective Principals as Identified by Emerging Leaders and Principals." *International Journal of Teacher Leadership* 2, no. 2 (Winter 2009): 39–48.

Mehta, Jal, Robert B. Schwartz, and Frederick M. Hess, eds. *The Futures of School Reform.* Cambridge, MA: Harvard Education Press, 2012.

Merseth, Katherine K. et al. *Inside Urban Charter Schools: Promising Practices and Strategies in Five High-Performing Schools.* Cambridge, MA: Harvard Education Press, 2009.

Murphy, Joseph. *Connecting Teacher Leadership and School Improvement.* Thousand Oaks, CA: Corwin Press, 2005.

Payne, Charles M. *So Much Reform, So Little Change: The Persistence of Failure in Urban Schools.* Cambridge, MA: Harvard Education Press, 2008.

Peske, Heather G. et al. "The Next Generation of Teachers: Changing Conceptions of a Career in Teaching." *Phi Delta Kappan* 83, no. 4 (2001): 304–311.

Ravitch, Diane. *The Death and Life of the Great American School System.* New York: Basic Books, 2010.

Reyes, Pedro, Jay D. Scribner, and Alicia P. Scribner. *Lessons from High-Performing Hispanic Schools: Creating Learning Communities.* New York: Teachers College Press, 1999.

Rothstein, Richard, Rebecca Jacobsen, and Tamara Wilder. *Grading Education: Getting Accountability Right.* New York: Teachers College Press & Economic Policy Institute, 2008.

Sahlberg, Pasi. *Finnish Lessons: What Can the World Learn from Educational Change in Finland?* New York: Teachers College Press, 2010.

Sobol, Thomas. *My Life in School: A Memoir.* New York: Public Schools for Tomorrow, 2013.

Stoelinga, Sara R., and Melinda M. Mangin. *Examining Effective Teacher Leadership: A Case Study Approach.* New York: Teachers College Press, 2012.

Troen,Vivian, and Katherine C. Boles. *Who Is Teaching Your Children? Why the Teacher Crisis Is Worse Than You Think and What Can Be Done About It?* New Haven, CT: Yale University Press, 2003.

———. *The Power of Teacher Teams.* Thousand Oaks, CA: Corwin Press, 2012.

ABOUT THE AUTHOR

AFTER SEVERAL YEARS as a community organizer with Mothers for Adequate Welfare, Marya R. Levenson began her educational career in 1971 as a ninth-grade history and civics teacher at the William Barton Rogers Junior High School in the Boston Public Schools (BPS). She was part of the team that created Madison Park High School, a magnet school, during Boston's desegregation era. Active in the Boston Teachers Union, she served on the BTU executive committee. In 1979–1980, in her capacity as staff associate to the superintendent, Levenson initiated the first BPS Middle Schools Task Force.

Levenson earned her EdD in administration and social policy from the Harvard Graduate School of Education (HGSE), where she became the assistant director of The Principals' Center. She was principal of Newton North (Massachusetts) High School from 1982 to 1990, and superintendent of the North Colonie (New York) School District from 1990 to 2001. She has served as president of the HGSE Alumni Council, a member of the Executive Committee of the New York State Council of School Superintendents, codirector of Public Schools for Tomorrow, and a member of the Editorial Advisory Board for the *Harvard Education Letter*. The New York State Council of School Superintendents recognized her service to students and schools in 1999, and in 2000 she received a Woman of Excellence award from the Albany-Colonie Regional Chamber of Commerce.

Since 2001, Levenson has been the Professor of the Practice in Education and the Harry S. Levitan Director of Education at Brandeis University, where she received the Louis Dembitz Brandeis Prize for Excellence in Teaching. She has written about assessments, school change, and student expectations.

Marya R. Levenson is married to Andy Hawley; between them, they have three children with spouses, five terrific grandchildren, and a beagle.

INDEX